"You Know who your Real Friends Are when your Back's Against the wall"

Dee Jones

Presents
Poetic
Thoughts of a
Federal A.I.C
Adult in Custody
Darryl "Bottega Boy Dee" Jones

Table of Content

A Harlem Night Rhythm
The City of Brother Love
Hope Revised
Another Kind of Concrete
The Blueprint of A Man
The Instant Connection
Where Our Colors Meet
Second Chance
A Familiar Ghost
Her Own Nightmare
The Measure of A Mistake
Faith of The Bronx
A Father's Return
One Voice
Still My Baby
The House of Strangers
Eric Dickerson
My Own Kind of Miracle
A Love That Distance Can't Break
His Harlem Flower
The Mending
Forever A King
Innocence Behind The Hood

Dedication

This book is dedicated to the Men & women behind the walls that have not found the ability to express the way they feel so these are my thoughts, no these are your thoughts, no better yet these are our thoughts written down by one, but voiced by many.. To the many people I came in contact with behind the wall I will be that Voice to express how you are feeling & just know you are not forgotten One love.

All poems & short stories are written By Bottega Boy Dee jones

Poetic thoughts of a Federal A.I.C (Adult in custody)

SPECIAL SHOUT-OUTS & THANK YOUS:

First I'd like to thank my lord and savior,
my Provider, my Protector, my Source.
Thank You for keeping me focused when my back was against the wall and everyone was praying on my down fall and for trusting me with this assignment,
To my fiance for forcing me to tap into my many skills, for having my back, putting up with my bullshit and taking care of our Son Although times were hard you still pushed through,
I'd like to give thanks to a special person that goes by the name of Panada my day one who knew me since sandbox days for putting up with my nonsense and helping me publish this book,
I'd like to give a special thanks to all my children,
To All My Real Rights Who's Behind The Wall, My Guy Uno, Latti, My Boy Shiest B aka Chin From Wilbur Section NJ, Wolverine Tone From Pink Houses, and my boy Sincere,
To My Real Rights On The Streets, My Second Family Bottega Boys, Mama Boy Productions, Tango,The Real Pop From The Barbershop, Skeem, International P, Brisk from Allen Town, Qua Wiliams my sister, Police Officer Michael Daniels aka Sunny, And Special Thanks To My Editor Terry For Critiquing My Work
And to all the people who pushed me, supported me, challenged me, and celebrated me — this is for you.
Thank you for seeing greatness in me even when I couldn't see it in myself.
Your support was the fuel.
Your belief was the foundation.
Your love was the breakthrough

Out of Sight, Out of Mind

Bottega Boy Dee

They slammed that cell, the echo rang,
Steel on steel, like freedom's chain.
A number now, not even a name,
And everything outside just ain't the same.
The phone don't ring like it used to do,
Messages dried up, letters too.
They swore they'd ride, they swore they'd write—
But silence is louder than any fight.
Mama prayed, but now she's tired,
My girl moved on, heart rewired.
Bros I bled for, left me behind,
Guess I learned—out of sight, out of mind.
Four cold walls and a ticking clock,
Time moves slow when the world don't talk.
The days all blur, the nights feel long,
Tryna stay sane, try to stay strong.
I replay laughs from back in the day,
The ones who said they'd never stray.
But loyalty's rare when life gets real,
They forget you fast behind that steel.
But I ain't broke, just bent a bit,
Mind still sharp, I ain't gonna quit.
One day I'm free, and when I shine,
I'll remember who stayed, and who declined.
'Cause even caged, I still can climb,
But it's cold here...
Out of sight, out of mind

Man in the SHU

Bottega Boy Dee

He was a family man, hard work in his soul,
Hands built callus from reaching his goals.
Clock in, clock out — no shame in the grind,
A man of his word, no slack in his mind.
Then one bad turn — metal met street,
Motorcycle down, life skipped a beat.
Bills kept coming, pain took hold,
But he still stood tall, still played bold.
Then came a call — a security check,
A short-term gig, a way to collect.
He thought, "If I play this smart, make my move right,
I can stack that bag, keep my fam in sight."
But one wrong step turned plans to chains,
A quick cash dream brought months of pain.
Steel doors slammed, cold world inside,
No room for weakness, no place to hide.
In that yard, respect's a must,
No paperwork? Then they don't trust.
He told his girl, "It's politics, babe —
Without proof, you sink, no one gets saved."
But she ain't get it, brushed it away,
Said she'd handle it — another day.
Papers never came, whispers grew loud,
They threw him in SHU, alone, no crowd.
Six long months — just him and his thoughts,
Battling' demons that peace forgot.
Verbal abuse, the cold, the pain,
Fighting' to hold onto his name.
He wrote her letters, heart on display,
"Please, just send what I need today."
But her pen slowed down, her tone got cold,
Said, "I'm teaching you a lesson — you'll learn, be bold."

Little did she know, inside that cell,
He was He was learning' lessons deep as hell.
Learning' who's real, who fades away,
Who writes back, and who just prays.
He learned that silence can cut like knives,
That love can die but the soul survives.
When the door cracked open, six months gone,
He walked out different — scarred, but strong.
Now he moves quiet, reads every sign,
Trusts in God, but guards his mind.
From a crash to a cage, he made it through,
but not the one she knew

Empire's Descent's.

Bottega Boy Dee

Chapter 1: The King's Demise

Harlem was in a state of silence, a thick midnight hush that had fallen upon it like a shroud. King Dejuan "DJ" Harlem, the notorious kingpin who had ruled the streets with an iron fist and a mind for strategy, was dead. An untimely, abrupt end to a swath of power that had reigned for decades, leaving the concrete kingdom shrouded in uncertainty and fear.

The sirens from earlier had stopped, leaving the night dark and still. People whispered behind closed doors, wondering, fearing who would step up, who would fall. For the empire that King DJ had built did not crumble with him; it loomed over the city, waiting.

Chapter 2: Divided Legacy

As the first light of dawn broke, two heirs stood before a gilded casket. They were twins, separated by mere ten minutes but a chasm of upbringing and ideology.

Azar Jones, King DJ's firstborn by those vital ten minutes, stood with a stoic silence befitting his education and station. He had been schooled in the finest colleges, had learned from business moguls and legal masterminds. His mother, Deanna, had raised him with one purpose—to legitimize the illegitimate, to transform the dark legacy of the Harlem streets into a dynasty of lawful power. Azar held his mother's ambition in his eyes, a spark of something that could be brilliance or ruin.

Afia, his sister, was of another world entirely. The streets had whispered her name long before this day. Raised in the underbelly of the empire, tutored in deception, manipulation, and raw power, she was her father's daughter in spirit and intent. Their mother, recognizing the fire in Afia's veins, had tempered it with harsh lessons on survival and dominance. As Afia stood there, draped in black, those who knew her saw not mourning, but a coronation.

Chapter 3: Mother's Aspirations Later in the gold-draped drawing room, Deanna Jones surveyed her offspring with a calculated gaze. The empire was at stake, and she was not about to let it falter. Deanna had lived through the grit of Harlem's rise and fall, had stood by Du's side and molded their children for this very moment. Azar was her pride, her ambition given form. She envisioned boardrooms and legitimate ventures seeded with the capital of old sins.

Afia, on the other hand, was her unbridled passion, a testament to her belief that power did not change, only shifted hands. Afia was ready, had been ready-she was Harlem's pulse, and Deanna knew that the streets would bow to one of their own.

"We are due more than this," Deanna would say to them both, "and you two are the key to it all."

Chapter 4: A Kingdom In Turmoil

The death of a king is the birth of chaos. King DJ's absence tore a rift through Harlem's underworld, and factions emerged from the shadows. Eyes turned to the heirs. Deals brokered in darkness came to light, promises made that were now called in question. Azar and Afia circled each other, bound by blood but separated by their visions for the future.

Azar met with lawyers, financiers, and anyone who could take the stained money and wash it through the markets. A new age of prosperity, he reasoned, could rise from the ashes of his father's empire.

Afia walked the streets, her loyalists gathering like storm clouds. She knew the codes, the loyalties bought with blood and fear.

"Harlem doesn't need a boardroom," she would whisper, "it needs a queen."

Chapter 5: Crossroad As the days bled into nights, the moment of choice loomed. Azar and Afia were the two pillars on which the fate of Harlem rested. Could they forge a new path together, or would their dueling ideologies tear apart the very fabric of their world? Sex, greed, drugs, and the manipulations of their mother wove a complex web. Rumors of betrayal, of alliances with fo Harlem on the brink swirled around them. Azar found himself torn between the temptation of power and the yearning for a clean legacy. Afia saw her birthright within reach but hesitated at the thought of what it would mean to seize it fully.

In the heart of Harlem, in the silence of decisions made in the dead of night, the heirs of King DJ would find their answers, and with them, the future of an empire.

Black & Endangered

By Bottega Boy Dee

Black skin, bold soul, born to survive,
But every breath feel like a risk to stay alive.
Melanin rich like the roots of the earth,
But they treat us like we lesser from the moment of birth.
We kings, we queens, we built this land,
Yet we walk with targets they don't understand.
Our strength they fear, our pride they shame,
We die for nothing, yet they call it "just the game."
Hands up — still shot.
Knees bent — still caught.
Speaking truth — still mocked.
Existence alone — still fought.
They see a hoodie, think "thief."
See a protest, call it "grief."
See us rise, they cut us low,
Planting cages where our gardens grow.
We march, we cry, we bleed, we pray,
But justice keeps looking the other way.
It's hard to dream when the sky feels closed,
When your color is a sentence and the judge already knows.
But we still rise — ain't that a wonder?
With rhythm in our walk and voices like thunder.
We still dance, still love, still build, still teach,
Still spread wisdom this world can't reach.
We are not the threat — we are the light,
But being Black means staying ready to fight.
Endangered, yes — but never extinct,
We the ink in history's deepest link.
So say it loud, let it be known:
We sacred, we powerful, we carved from stone.
And even if they fear what we embody,
Being Black is a blessing not a body.

He Never Blocked His Blessings

He carried many problems
like stones inside his coat,
heavy on his shoulders
but he never once lost hope.
Life hit him with the hard days,
the long nights, the tight corners,
but he kept stepping forward—
a quiet, standing warrior.
Folks wondered how he did it,
how he stayed so steady still,
but he learned long ago
that faith walks farther than will.
So he opened every door he could,
even when his own were closing,
gave his last to someone else
when his pockets weren't overflowing.
He didn't block his blessings,
not with anger, not with pride,
he kept his heart wide open
and let the light inside.
Because he knew what you give
comes back in its own timing,
and even in the stormy moments
something greater was designing.
So he paid it forward always—
small kindnesses, big sacrifices,
and somehow every broken path
still led him to rising.
A man with many troubles,
but a spirit that never bent—
for he lived by one simple truth:
a blessing shared is never spent.

Can't Block His Blessings

He had problems stacked on problems,
life hit him like a storm with no warning,
but every time the weight got heavy,
he still stood up in the morning.
A lot of folks would've folded,
slid back, or lost direction—
but he kept his spirit open,
never blocking his own blessings.
See, he walked through pain quiet,
never cried for no attention,
'cause he knew real strength is shown
in choices, not in mentions.
Even when his pockets hurting,
even when his plans fell through,
he still gave what he could give—
that's just what real ones do.
He paid it forward every time:
the rides, the favors, the meals,
the prayers whispered for others
while battling his own ordeals.
He didn't let pride choke him,
didn't let anger cloud his vision,
he moved with a humble purpose—
heart clean, soul on a mission.
And somehow, through the struggle,
through the losses, through the lessons,
doors kept opening for him
'cause he never blocked his blessings.
A man built from hard days,
but molded by compassion—
living proof you rise higher
when you lift others with your actions.

He Kept His Blessings Moving

He came up with problems
that didn't wait their turn—
they hit all at once,
stacked high, let the whole world burn.
Bills late.
Trust broke.
Family pulling both sides.
Trying to heal a heart
that stayed bruised from old tides.
But even with the stress on his back,
and the world calling him worthless,
he walked like a man who knew
God don't waste a purpose.
He could've turned cold,
shut down, pushed everyone away—
but he had a heart that refused
to move dirty or stray.
See, he never blocked his blessings,
not with bitterness, not with fear.
He kept his circle small
but his spirit crystal clear.
When he had a dollar,
he gave fifty cents to someone hurting worse.
When he had nothing at all,
he still spoke life instead of a curse.
People used him,
lied on him,
left him out in the cold—
but he stayed the same man,
never traded kindness for gold.
He paid it forward every chance,
even when life cut him deep—
knew the seeds you plant today

are the ones your soul will reap.
And that's why doors cracked open
that no man could shut—
why he kept rising out the trenches
when others stayed stuck.
A man with heavy problems,
but a heart too strong for stressing—
'cause he knew every storm he survived
was just making room
for the next blessing.
A quiet war he never confessed.
The world saw calm in his steady stride,
But carried pain he kept tucked inside.

A Man Who Gave Despite the Weight

He walked with storms inside his chest,Still, every morning he rose with grace,
A tired smile on a weathered face.
For though his burdens bent him low,
He found a way to let kindness grow.
He'd buy a meal for a stranger in line,
Say, "Keep your change, you'll be fine."
Hold open doors, give up his seat,
Lift heavy bags for tired feet.
He patched small holes in other hearts,
While his own was tearing apart.
Never once did he let it show—
He'd lace his wounds and still help folks glow.
He believed blessings weren't meant to hoard,
That love was the only true reward.
So even on nights he felt undone,
He lit someone else's world like a rising sun.
A man of struggle, a man of grace—
Who carried hope to every place.
For the kindest souls, the world should know,
Are often the ones still healing as they go.

He Gave What He Didn't Have

He moved like a man stitched together
from long nights and quiet battles—
a little worn, a little weary,
but still standing on faith
like it was the only solid ground he knew.
Life had him bent but not broken,
carrying troubles he never named,
struggles that sat heavy on his chest
like unpaid bills and unspoken prayers.
But even then—
even when the world pressed him down—
he found space in his heart
to lift somebody else.
He was the type who'd see a mother counting change
and slide a twenty across the counter
before she could finish apologizing.
The type who'd stop for the old man
stranded with a dead battery
though his own tank was running on fumes.
He gave rides in the rain,
gave advice without judgment,
gave smiles when he barely had the strength
to hold his own together.
He'd say, "A blessing ain't a blessing
if you keep it locked in your pocket."
There were nights he'd go home
and sit in the dark,
wondering when his turn would come—
when someone might show up
to help him carry his load.
But he never let that bitterness grow.
He believed kindness was a seed you planted
even when you didn't know

if you'd live long enough to see it sprout.
People felt lighter around him,
like their problems shrank
just by sharing space with his quiet strength.
He listened the way the sky listens to thunder—
patient, steady, without flinching.
And even when his own heart
was cracking like old wood,
he kept showing up
with gentleness in his hands.
Some called him soft.
Some called him strange.
But those who truly saw him—
they knew the truth:
that it takes a different kind of courage
to give what you don't have,
to pour from a cup
you've been patching with hope and prayer.
One day, somebody asked him,
"Why you always helping folks
when you got your own storms to fight?"
He just smiled, tired but sincere,
and said,
"Because somebody out there
got it worse than me.
And if I can be the reason
they breathe a little easier—
just for a moment—
then maybe my own pain
ain't for nothing."
And so he walked on,
not perfect, not painless,
but powerful in a quiet, holy way—
a reminder that the world
still has men who choose light

even when they're standing in the dark.
A man who carried kindness
like armor.
A man who stayed giving
even when life tried
to take everything from him.
A man who proved you don't need much
to be a blessing—
just a heart that refuses
to stop shining.

The Man Who Threw Stones at the Pen

By Bottega Boy Dee

He walked with a chip sittin' high on his shoulder,
The heart grew colder as the world grew older.
Swore he'd never fold, never let 'em win—
So he kept throwin' stones at the federal pen.
Every time they said, "Boy, slow it down,"
He sped up, ridin' dirty through town.
Told himself, "I'm just tryna eat,"
But hunger doesn't justify life in the streets.
The block was hot, his soul ran cold,
Every lick hit, every brick sold.
Eyes on him, but he ain't care when—
He was too busy throwin' stones at the pen.
Warnings came like the wind in the trees,
OGs spoke, but he ain't heed.
"Son, that cage got a bed with your name,"
But pride don't bend when you deep in the game.
Court dates came like shadows at night,
He played it cool, never showing his fright.
But deep down knew it was catchin' up,
The system doesn't sleep and the judge doesn't bluff.
Now he sits in a cell with a thousand regrets,
Letters unread, cold silhouette.

Thought he was a king, too raw to bend—
But the pen doesn't break, and it always wins.
So if you out there thinkin' you can't fall,
Too slick, too quick, above it all—
Just know that pride can wear thin,
When you spend your youth throwin' stones at the pen.

A Letter to My Old Self

By Bottega Boy Dee
Dear Me,
The one who moved too fast to see,
Who thought the world was enemy,
Who wore pain like it was pride,
And let the hurt just burn inside—
I see you now, young, wild, and blind,
Chasing shadows, losing time.
You laughed loud just to hide the cries,
You trusted fake love, believed the lies.
You thought being hard was how to cope,
Took every fall and called it hope.
But deep down, you were just a boy
Trying to turn that hurt into some joy.
I wish I could've told you then,
Not every battle need be fought to win.
That silence don't make you weak or soft,
And real ones never write you off.
I would've told you: slow your pace,
There's more to life than just the race.
That scars can heal, and pain won't last,
But you gotta let go of that heavy past.
You ain't gotta prove your worth through war,
You deserve peace, and so much more.
And love? It starts from deep within—

Not from streets or liquor or sins.
But even through the wrong you chose,
You made it here, bruised but bold.
You still stand, you still survive—
And in your eyes, I see I'm alive.
So to the old me, with love and pain,
Thank you for walking through the rain.
You made mistakes, but you made me too—
And I promise now, I'll carry you.
Sincerely,
The man you grew to be.
Free in spirit, finally... me.

A hazy day in April

Amidst the April days so green, There lies a date, quite well-seen, April's twentieth, clear and bold, A time when stories are often told.

Four-two-zero, digits align, Symbolic of a culture's sign, A code for those who take to flight, On smoldering wings into the night.

Whispers of the herb so sweet,

Gatherings where enthusiasts meet, Laughter rings, eyes glisten bright, In the camaraderie of the light.

Clouds of comfort, tendrils rise,

Shapes they form in smoke-filled skies,

Earthy fragrance fills the air, A signal of the ritual there.

For some, it's peace, for others jest, A moment's freedom from life's quest, In unity, they share this time,A clockwork of the perennial chime.

From shire to city, they come to share, The bonding over a leaf so fair, In joy and jest, they find their kin, Inhaling deep, the state they re in.

Not a nod to nations, but to a plant, In the simple leaf, complex enchant,

As the clock strikes upon the hour, A marked tradition shows its power.

Four twenty's call, a tranquil roar, Of natural bond, folklore, and more, Celebrating in their own way,

The timeless dance of night and day.

So pause and notice this worldly span, Where for a moment, time's gears jam, And every soul with glee partakes, In the camaraderie that four-two-zero makes.

The Reckoning of the Fast Life

Once upon a time in the bustling streets of West Philly, there was a 20-year-old named Malik. He had earned himself a reputation as a scammer, and to be honest, he was good at it. Malik's block was "doing numbers," as he'd put it, because the neighborhood folks knew him as the guy who could hustle money out of thin air. His crew looked up to him; after all, he was making cash hand over fist and living the lavish life they all dreamed of.

Malik decked himself out in what he claimed were outfits that cost thousands, with flashy sneakers to match. His aura oozed confidence, and that swagger made him stand out on his block. But Malik's life took an unexpected turn one day when he and his boys decided it would be cool to boost a johny'—street slang for a stolen car. They had pulled off scams before, but this was their first dive into grand theft auto.

Predictably, their joyride ended with blaring sirens and flashing lights. The arrest was a hit to Malik's ego, but not a knockout. He was confident that his street smarts and slick talking would get him out of trouble. And initially, it looked like he was right—he managed to beat the case. Thinking he'd dodged a bullet, Malik strutted out of the courtroom like he owned the pavement beneath his feet.

But freedom was short-lived. The feds had their eyes on Malik too, and they weren't just interested in a stolen car. They'd been building a case against him for his other illicit activities. Before he knew it, Malik was wearing cuffs again, this time with charges he couldn't charm his way out of.

Once inside the federal penitentiary, Malik quickly realized the rules of the street didn't apply. His notoriety meant nothing here.

Inmates dealt with him not out of respect, but out of necessity. After all, Malik was Muslim, and the code of brotherhood extended to him,

if only just.

His downfall began when his sneakers, the same ones he flaunted on the outside, were snatched right from under his bunk.

The thief strutted around the day room in them, and while everyone noticed, Malik didn't dare ask for them back. His pride, once impenetrable, had been shattered.

Whispers turned into loud talks, with stories of Malik's supposed wealth unravelling fast. When photo day came, and his

"blinged-out" image was expected to shine, the reality was laid bare. His outfit was modest at best, estimated at a mere $300 to $400. Inmates smelled the lie; they sensed the facade crumbling.

Malik became the laughingstock. Inmates dished out advice, sharing the concept of humility with him, but their words fell on deaf ears. He clung to his tales of wealth, insisting that once he got to his "compound" - a term inmates use for their next designation in the prison system - he would show them all how a

real hustler leveled up.

But the truth was, Malik was no longer the big fish in a small pond. He was just another inmate, holding onto the frayed edges of a past life, a life that now seemed as counterfeit as the scams he used to run. If he was going to survive, Malik knew deep down he had to adapt and reinvent himself, not with flashy clothes or tall tales, but with respect, resilience, and perhaps, a dose of the humility everyone kept talking about.

Afia, My First Born

Afia S. Jones, my precious, my light,
I've stumbled at times, I ain't always been right.
The years have been heavy, distance too long,
But love for you, daughter, has always stayed strong.
I know I've been missing, not near as I should,
If I could turn back, I promise I would.
Not gifts from the store, not silver, not gold,
But words from my heart, the truth I now hold.
On this day, your birthday, your moment to shine,
I give you this poem, a piece that is mine.
It's all that I have, but it's honest and true,
A father's first prayer is always for you.
I'm trying, my baby, to make a new way,
To show up, to guide you, to brighten your days.
Forgive what I lacked, see the love that I send,
My daughter, my blessing, my heart without end.
Happy Birthday, Afia, may your spirit stay strong,
Your story is precious, your journey lifelong.
And no matter the miles, the years, or the strife,
You'll always be the brightest part of my life.

Strength from the unseen

Once upon a time in a shadow-clad corner of a bustling city, there lived a young girl named Ava. Her childhood was shattered one harrowing night when she witnessed the brutal murder of her parents. A notorious drug dealer and pimp, known on the streets as "The Viper," was the orchestrator of this nightmare.

Young Ava, hiding in the dark recesses of her closet, saw it all through the slats of the door—a view that would taint her vision of the world forever. The smell of gunpowder and fear mingled in the cramped space as she stifled her sobs. Tears carved rivers of sorrow on her face, yet she uttered not a sound. She dared not move until the haunting silence reassured her that the Viper and his henchmen had slinked back into the night

.

Ava emerged into a world devoid of the warmth and safety that most children take for granted. From that night onward, her life became a sequence of foster homes and youth shelters, each move washing away parts of her former life, but never the stain of that night's terror.

Ava grew to be fiercely independent and exceptionally resilient. She channeled her grief into a relentless pursuit of justice, vowing to herself that she would never let the weak suffer as she had. Yet her heart harbored a dark coal of vengeance, buried deep beneath the surface of her day-to-day life.

She became a criminal psychologist, specializing in the apprehension of those who lived in the underworld that had claimed her parents. Her work led her to witness the cruelty of humanity, but nothing could prepare her for the full circle her life would soon take.

Two decades after the night that changed everything, a new case landed on Ava's desk. It involved a high-ranking officer with purported ties to the very criminal elements he was sworn to dismantle. Detective Lucas Bennett was his name, revered by many, yet whispered about in suspect circles.

Ava pored over the files with meticulous attention. As she matched past crimes with present information, a chilling realization crept up her spine. Patterns began to emerge, and within these patterns hid a face-a face she had spent nights reconstructing from childhood memories. It was him. Lucas Bennett was the Viper. The merciless young dealer had metamorphosed into a figure of the law.

Her heart raced with a mixture of dread and vindication. It was as if the past had risen to claim retribution. She could not allow her emotions to cloud her judgment; she needed proof, concrete proof that Bennett was the monster from her past.

Ava embarked on a silent crusade, meticulously tracing Bennett's activities and unearthing the evidence that bound him to the nefarious deeds of his former life. With each passing day, the line between the hunter and the hunted seemed to blur.

Then fate forced the confrontation she had longed for and feared. A community event to honor the police force placed Ava in the same room as Bennett. Their eyes met across the crowd—his, glinting with the arrogance of the powerful; hers, burning with the intensity of her untamed past.

"You look familiar," Bennett remarked casually, extending his hand. "Have we met before?"

Ava collected herself, her voice even. "Perhaps in another life, Detective."

She knew she had to tread carefully, for accusing a man of Bennett's stature without definitive proof could be career suicide.. and possibly real suicide.

The cat-and-mouse game between Ava and Bennett continued. The more she pursued the truth, the more dangerous her quest became. And yet Ava's sharp mind matched her will of iron. She connected dots where others saw only random splatters of a chaotic underworld.

Finally, the breakthrough came—a long-forgotten piece of evidence resurfaced, irrefutably linking Bennett to the night Ava had become an orphan. The mask of law-abiding citizen Bennett wore so well was about to crumble.

Ava watched from the shadows of the courtroom as Bennett was brought to justice. As he attempted to defend himself, all gloss and blind assurance, streetwise security guards cuffed him. The court saw through his facade, stripping him of his honor and freedom

'This isn't over," Bennett hissed as he was led away, his gaze slicing through the courtroom to find Ava.

But Ava felt a weight lift from her shoulders. She had faced her past head-on and emerged victorious. Justice, not vengeance, would be her legacy

. Bennett would no longer prey on the susceptible, no longer shadow the lives of innocents. And Ava, standing tall amidst the ruins of her darkest night, knew her life had indeed come full circle; not as a circle of never-ending despair, but as one that spiraled upward into hope and a future unclouded by the ghosts of her past.

The love story unfolds

In the small coastal town of Sea bridge lay nestled a quaint, sun-drenched street lined with cherry blossom trees, where a man named Charlie lived, holding onto a love that was fraying at the seams. He was an ordinary man, with large, calloused hands and a face that carried the soft smile of contentment. A seal of commitment encircled his finger, a promise forged with the love of his life, Sophia

.

Sophia, with her cascading chestnut hair and eyes like the twilight sky, was the woman who had captured Charlie's heart in a whirlwind romance that felt like it belonged in a fairy tale. They shared dreams of a future together: a cozy home, the laughter of children, and years entwined in each other's arms

.

As their wedding day approached, however, shadows from Charlie's past began to stretch into their present. Although Charlie had long since turned a new leaf, his bachelor days of youthful folly and indiscretions had left marks that time had not fully erased.. Sophia, plagued by insecurities, found herself unable to shake the haunting tales of Charlie's earlier escapades, tales whispered by the gossip of small-town tongues that refused to lie silent

.

Every time Sophia's fear surfaced, it came as an icy dagger of doubt. Whispered conversations at the local diner became sly glances at a presumed flirtation. Laughter shared with an old female friend became a heart-twisting jealousy. With every finger that Sophia pointed, Charlie's heart sank a little more. He professed his innocence, his fidelity, his unwavering commitment to the love they had cultivated

.

"I'm not the man I was," Charlie would tell her, his voice a mix of resolve and weariness. "I'm here, with you, for you. There's nothing I want more than to move forward, hand in hand, leaving the past where it belongs."

But the specter of history is a formidable foe, and despite his earnest pleas, Sophia's fears persisted, each accusation tightening the noose around their happiness. The warmth in their home turned to a chill, the laughter to silence.

The wedding dress hanging in the closet, a symbol of their unity, now seemed to mock the distance growing between them

.

Charlie's heart ached as he watched the love of his life drown in a sea of distrust. He yearned to reach out, to guide her to the shores of trust once more, but each attempt felt like winds against a tempest. Listless days turned into restless nights as the once-clear path to matrimony became littered with the debris of past mistakes

.

Then one day, as the cherry blossoms began to fall like snowflakes upon the street, Charlie stood before the bedroom mirror, the specter of his former self staring back. He had struggled in the tempest of Sophia's doubt, tethered his heart to a mast that groaned under the weight of her suspicions. His love remained steadfast, but even the stoutest ship could only weather so many storms

.

Feeling his spirit ebb with each passing moment, he came to the hardest decision of his life. He sat down, took pen to paper, and let his heart bleed into words, words that were the marriage of pain, hope, and an unwavering love.

"Sophia," he wrote, "I have loved you since the moment I saw you, and I have dreamt of our life together every day since. But love is like a garden that must be tended to with trust as its lifeblood. Without it, the most beautiful flowers wither. I am laying my soul bare to you, placing my heart in your hands, hoping that you can see the man I am now, rather than the shadows of who I once was."

"I have been faithful to you, to us. If our future is to flourish, we need to cultivate it with understanding, forgiveness, and faith. I ask you, my love, to look deep within your heart, to find the strength to trust in the man who stands before you now, who cherishes every moment with you."

Sophia found the letter on the kitchen table, the ink barely dry, next to a simple bouquet of wildflowers. Her hands trembled as she read the words that seemed to echo through the very walls of their home.

Faced with the raw truth of her own fears and the depth of Charlie's love, tears streamed down her cheeks. In that moment, a clear choice lay before her:

to continue to be chained to the remnants of a past long dead or to embrace the man Charlie had become.

The journey was not an easy one... Forgiveness does not bloom overnight, and trust is a delicate flower that needs time to open fully to the sun. Yet Sophia knew that her path forward was intertwined with Charlie's, that the love they shared was worth every effort to uphold

.

Threading her fingers through Charlie's, Sophia looked into his eyes, which held a storm of hope and apprehension, and whispered the three words that began the healing of their hearts: "I trust you."

As they moved through the tempest, the pointing fingers became handholds of support, the memories of mistrust faded, and the echoes of the past grew silent. It was a journey taken one step at a time, a story of a man and woman who learned that true love is a fortress built not just upon the joys of the present but also upon the forgiveness of the past

.

They stood together beneath the cherry blossoms the following spring, vows exchanged not just in the presence of friends and family, but also in the presence of their own strengthened bond. The air was rich with the scent of renewal and the promise that trust, once firmly rooted, can weather any storm and blossom into a love that endures.

WAIT ON NO MAN

Upon the endless march of hours,

Where sunrise blooms and midnight glowers,

A truth as steady as the land, Proclaims that time waits on no man.

It breezes through the infant's coo, And races past the aged, too,Its footprints etched upon the sands, Confirm that time waits on no man.

The tides of seconds ebb and flow, Past moments lost we'll never know.The clock unwinds its lifelong span, For time, it waits on no man.

We cast our dreams into its stream, And chase them 'neath the moonlight gleam.But still, against our fervent plan, Alas, time waits on no man.

The young may sprint, the old may stroll, Still, onward goes time's silent toll, Unseen it wings across our span, For time, it waits on no man.

The rich may plead, the poor demand, In every clime, in every land, Yet none escape the cosmic ban, Immutable, time waits on no man.

So seize the day, embrace the night, Hold loved ones close,

make wrongs aright,

Time's symphony has but one strand, The stark refrain: it waits on no man.

With wisdom's voice or folly's din,

Soon ends the race that none can win.

Let's love and live while still we can, As through the glass slips every grain;

Behold the truth, both clear and plain—

Time's tide waits on no man.

Confessions of a friend

In the realm of connection, beyond the hearts pure sway, Lies a bond quite different, in shades of night and day

There with the taste of friendship, sweet and ever so light, Lurk whispers of desire, veiled in the cloak of night.

Beneath the guise of laughter, and shared, innocuous grins, Pulses surge clandestine, as subtle yearning begins.

A venture bold, unspoken, where emotions lie in wait, Two friends embark on a path, to a tempting, furtive state.

In the glow of moon's soft luminescence, secrets are shared, Where the currency of touch, is the only fare that's dared.

Entangled in a dance of need, where pleasure's the only end, Two souls seek solace and release, in the arms of a friend.

No promise of tomorrow, in this fleeting, tender game, They find solace in the silence, that speaks each other's name.

With the morning's light, they return to the chaste day's light, Yet know when dusk embraces, again they'll unite in the night.

But oh, tread cautiously, dear hearts, who mingle flesh with fun, For the weaving of such webs can be easily undone.

The heart, a fragile traveler, might find a hopeful dream, In the maze of 'benefits,' things are not all as they seem.

To seek warmth in another, without the binds of love, Requires understanding, and respect thereof.

May joy be found in moments, in caresses, sweet and brief, Yet remember, with the pleasure, sometimes comes the grief.

So here's to friends with secrets, in the dance of push and pull, May they navigate their passion, with a heart that's wise and full.

May the fun remain unfettered, as they respect the rules they set, In the game of friends with benefits, where friendship's the safe

A joke in two parts

Laugh Now, Cry Later, masks of time's grand theatre, A paradox carved on life's silver platter.

A comedy, a tragedy, our dual feature,

Stitch scenes of joy and tears in the same matter.

Behind the curtain of the smiling face, Echoes silent sobs, a hidden river.

Yet, laughter rings, resonating with grace, Concealing shadows where our sorrows quiver.

Laugh now, oh heart, amidst the bright-lit stage, Where jesters dance and merry tunes do swell.

Embrace the light, let mirth your soul engage, Before the tolling of the evening bell.

For later, tears may trace a silken trail,

When stars are veiled and laughter seems to pale.

Cry later, in the quiet of the night, When the crowd departs and all the world's asleep.

No eyes to judge, no need for brave facade, Just raw emotion that you no longer keep.

A balance act, this play of life commands, To laugh, to cry, both sides of the same coin.

Today we stand with giggles in our hands, Tomorrow may from sorrow's cup we join.

So let us toast to both the joy and pain, For each gives measure to the other's gain.

In life's grand dance, keep step to this refrain:

Laugh now, cry later—love, loss, sunshine, rain

Correction officer H

Beneath the cosmic veil of night, she moves, A vision, shrouded in the mystic hues.

By "H" she is known, an enigma in bloom, Her beauty speaks in silent, perfumed tunes.

A scent so divine, like Eden's own air, Draws the soul to her, a wistful affair.

In her presence, the flowers seem to bow, For even nature reveres her scent's vow.

Her eyes, they are the stars' celestial pair, Twinkling with secrets, galaxies declare.

Orbs so radiant, dusk's own jewels shamed, In their gaze, hearts flutter, untamed.

A fateful encounter, not meant to be, Intrigued, we stand, on this boundary.

Protocols and lines, we do not cross, Yet in admiration, I am at a loss.

I am the silent guardian of my heart's creed,

Following the rules, where honor leads.

Yet, oh, to imagine a different scene, Where "H" and I could meet, without routine.

But for now, I respect where lines are drawn,

Admiring her light, like the breaking dawn.

If ever the universe shifts its design, Rewrites the rules that now confine,

Me l be there, a question poised in the night, To ask her out, where stars witness in delight.

To dine, to laugh, and to share in life's feast, Till then, I dream of her, from the west to the east.

h fates untold, There stood a man, brave and bold,Named Big Dee, strong and constant as the day, Witnessing from afar his daughter's play.

Afia, her name, a spirit bright,Grew up beneath life's ardent light, Seventeen summers swiftly passed, And in her heart, questions amassed.

Unknown to her, in shadows kept, Her father's gaze, it never slept.From distant realms, with quiet sigh, He watched her laugh, he heard her cry.

He marveled at her every stride,The lows, the highs, the roller-coaster ride, Each triumph, each stumble in her life's dance, From afar he cherished every chance..

Her laughter echoed in his ear, A balm to soothe the passing year, Big Dee a fortress of silent cheer, Keeping his bloodline close and dear.

Then came the day, as fate designed, Two lives, once split, were realigned.

Afia's gaze met Big Dee's own, In her eyes, the years overgrown.

"Daughter mine," he softly said,

"Through life's thickets, I've quietly tread.

Carrying hopes, bearing dreams,
Watching over you through unseen streams."
In her heart, where questions swirled, A space for him, slowly unfurled.
The puzzle of past, in pieces laid,
As father's presence cut through the shade.
Now together, hand in hand,
Rebuilding bridges long unmanned, Big Dee, with heart so full and wide,
Grateful to be by Afia's side.
For every chapter missed in fright, They turn the page, they reignite.
A father's love, once paused in time, Now sings aloud in life's grand rhyme.

The man who stood at the cross roads

heart's secluded chamber where the fire of love does burn, There resides a weary traveler, at a fateful, daunting turn.Two paths before him glisten, with the promise of the sun, A man, he stands divided, between two hearts, not one.

The first, a flame of passion, with a fierce and tempest glow, A wildflower wind, impulsive, where the reckless rivers flow.Her eyes, they dance with firelight, her spirit, unconfined, The man is lost within her, enchanted, and entwined.

The second path is gentle, like a soft and steady rain, A woman of quiet strength, whose love is not in vain.

Her touch, a soothing balm that calms the tempest within, A harbor safe and steadfast, amidst a world of din.

One love spins him in fervor, a dizzy, whirling flight, An orbit traced with fever, burning through the night.

She is his fiery comet, a blaze that shoots then fades, A story penned in passion, lined in fervent, bold tirades.

The other, constant as the stars, a glow that never wanes, A love that's deep and nurturing, run through by verdant veins.

Her heart, a steady beacon, alight with tender care, Her presence, warm and rekindling, a respite from despair.

Alas, this man, he wavers between the hearth and storm, By daylight, touched by one's calm, by night, by the other's form.Each woman, a hemisphere, his heart the battleground, A ceaseless dual of longings, where peace is seldom found.

In this tug-of-war of affection, where both love and pain reside, He wrestles with his destiny, with no place left to hide.Each choice is sweet and bitter, each path leads to some pain, For choosing one means losing—a love not had again.

So ponder, weary traveler, for only time will tell,

Which love will be your undoing, which heart in which you'll dwell.Is it the wild tempest's fury, or the quiet, steadfast truth, That will shape the man you're to become, in the waning days of youth?

He lingers in the throe's embrace, where two loves hold fast, And like the changing currents, he must choose at last.The road he'll journey onward, by one woman's side to stand, With a heart that's torn asunder in the realm of love's demand.

The son of Harlem

In Harlem's heart where dreams may fray, A single child walks the alley's play, No siblings' laughter or shared delight,

A solo flight in the city's night.

An only child in the urban maze, With stoops that echo the city's phase, Where jazz and sorrow are intertwined, A soul that dances, uniquely designed.

The tenement walls, they rise so high, Graffiti tales, under the sky,As bodegas share their spiced arrays, This child of Harlem paves new ways.Amidst the sirens and the concrete bloom, A solitary rose in the urban gloom, In playground kingdoms, rulers crowned, Yet in his realm, no kin is found.

The brownstones hold a thousand tales, Of lives entwined in this borough of veils, Yet in the crowd, he stands alone, One heart, one mind, a singular tone.Harlem whispers its ancient lore, Of Langston's dreams and so much more, This only child with eyes that gleam, Holds the neighborhood's solitary dream.

He wanders through the historic streets, Where every corner, past and future meets, A world of contrast, sharp and brash, Yet love and community, a vibrant clash.Amongst the chatter and the hustle's flow, An only child, where kinship grows, Not from blood, but shared strife,

The siblings of his urban life.So he marches forth with courage sound, In the ghetto of Harlem, he is bound.

To rise above, to claim his right, An only child, with a spirit bright.

A place known only to us

In the sanctum of whispers, where shadows merge,

Beneath the veil of night, passions surge.

Canvas of silence, broken with breaths, A symphony of touch, weaving through depths.

The ballet of heartbeats, a synchronized thrum, In the hush of the twilight, to desires succumb.

Two silhouettes dance, in the soft moon's glow, In the theatre of sheets, where secret loves flow.

Whispers like satin, glide in the air, In the rhythm of longing, a duet rare.

Gentle and fervent, the pace they dictate, In the kingdom of pillows, where love conjugates.

Eyes that speak volumes, in the dim-lit room, Embraces the canvas, dispels the gloom.

Sealed with a kiss, tender and profound,

In the embrace of dusk, where affections are crowned.

A crescendo rising, in the cloak of the night, Their universe shrinking, to a single point of light.

With the peak of pleasure, as stars applaud in action,

The bedroom becomes an ode to attraction.

In the aftermath, serene, a tranquil sea, Two lovers lie spent, in sweet tranquility.

Breath slows to whispers, hearts softly hum, Until dawn's light breaks, and night becomes mum.

Profile of a Predator

Once upon a time in Brooklyn, New York, there was a man named Gabriel Torrent. He was an enigma, with a quiet disposition and an unassuming appearance, yet inside him brewed a storm of dark impulses. Gabriel grew up in the digital era, a time when the world was interconnected through screens and social media platforms. But rather than use these tools to build bridges, Gabriel constructed a labyrinth of terror

.

As a child, Gabriel was often overlooked and neglected, his voice drowned out by the constant buzz of the city. He found solace in the anonymity of chat rooms and forums, where he could don a mask and be anyone he desired. But as time went on, the mask began to fuse with his skin, the lines between reality and the digital persona blurring.

When Gabriel reached adulthood, he was a man divided. By day he wandered the ever-busy Brooklyn streets, a ghost among the living. But by night, he soared across the digital landscape, his presence felt globally. Despite the countless interactions, Gabriel never formed true connections. That is until fleeting messages started to invade his solitude - curious internet denizens seeking connection, not knowing they were flirting with danger.

They called him "The Nomad," a name he embraced. To the world, it represented his love for travel, as he shared breathtaking images from cities around the globe. However, beneath the curated gallery of beautiful landscapes and exotic landmarks, there lurked a sinister agenda. The Nomad was on a hunt, not for sights, but for victims.

The pattern was always the same. He'd receive a direct message, a stray comment, or some form of digital outreach. But rather than reply with kindness or dismiss the interaction, Gabriel would meticulously research the person behind the screen. Utilizing his skills in hacking and social engineering, he unearthed addresses, routines, and, critically, when they would be most vulnerable.

His travels were a morbid tour with a dark purpose. He'd arrive in a new city, not to see the sights, but to stalk his prey—those unfortunate souls who had dared reach out to him casually, naively. He'd study them, follow them, and when the moment was just right, they would disappear, leaving behind a digital ghost where once there was a thriving presence.

The media dubbed him "The Social Media Killer." They reported on the shocking vanishings, the stark silences where once vibrant online personas had been. Fear swept across platforms as users began to question the potential horrors that might be lurking behind every friend request and direct message.

Yet, amidst the chaos, Gabriel felt an insatiable hunger growing. The thrill of the hunt was addictive, but it was also spiraling out of his control. He was no longer the puppeteer; he had become the puppet to his dark desires.

As his list of victims grew, so did the efforts to catch him. Digital forensics teams, international law enforcement agencies, and cybersecurity experts all worked in a frantic race against time to track down the elusive killer before he could strike again.

In the end, it was the very platform he had used to select his victims that became his downfall.

A meticulous pattern emerged from the data, a digital signature that he had inadvertently left behind. And when authorities finally caught up with Gabriel in a small cafe in Prague, the faces of his pursuers were not unlike the avatars of those he had once stalked: surreal, yet all too real.

Gabriel Torrent was brought to justice, his reign of terror brought to an abrupt halt. The world grew a little wiser, a little more cautious in the wake of his capture. Social media users began to embrace anonymity with respect, understanding the vulnerability that came with visibility.

The story of Gabriel Torrent, the man from Brooklyn who became a global predator, serves as a chilling reminder that behind the veil of digital interaction, reality remains, as does the potential for darkness. It's a tale that echoes through the tweets, posts, and updates, whispering to us to tread carefully in the vast, connected world we have built.

For Samaya

By Bottega Boy Dee

Her name is Samaya, a light in the storm,
A young Black queen in a world so torn.
But they didn't see beauty in her deep, rich shade,
Only mocked the skin that God Himself made.
"Too dark," they said, with a cruel little laugh,
As if her worth could be cut in half.
In school halls where whispers sting,
She walked alone, carrying everything.
She watched the lighter girls get praised,
While she stood in shadows, hurt and dazed.
Felt invisible in every crowd,
But held back tears, too proud to cry out loud.
They never knew the war she fought,
Or the heavy thoughts her silence brought.
Nights she stared at the ceiling light,
Wondering if she'd make it through the night.
"Why me?" she asked, with a voice so small,
"Why was I born to feel so small?"
And in the mirror, she wished away
The parts of her they threw away.
But, Samaya, let me tell you this—
You are made of roots and stars and bliss.
Your skin ain't dark, it's dipped in gold,
A story of queens and legends told.
You are the sun after heavy rain,
You are the proof that beauty grows through pain.
Don't let their hate rewrite your name,
You're not broken—you're just flame.
And if you ever feel alone again,
Remember this world don't define your end.
You're magic, baby, you're deep, divine—
You don't just survive, you rise and shine.

So let them talk, let them scoff,
Your crown was never meant to come off.
Samaya, you're more than enough, always were—
You are a darker hue of love,
And that... is power.

The cost of the ride

In the fading light of a Newark neighborhood , our girls who had grown up scaling the gritty pavements of their block shared an unusual bond-born not of whispers over dollhouses, but of the adrenaline rush that accompanied stealthily slipping into their parents' cars as children, the engines purring at their illicit touch. They were grown now, their child's play morphing into a risky gambit of adulthood. Their names whispered on the wind: Jasmine, Keira, Lola, and Tia.

They were an inconspicuous lot ,their smiles coy,their footsteps silent.to those neighbors they were sweet and precarious dreams twirling in their eyes. But beneath the soft facades were sharp minds, hardened by life in Newark's merciless streets. As kids, it was just a game. As adults, it was a livelihood. Their targets were the anonymous vehicles of the city, plucked from the indifferent streets to be disappeared into the bowels of a local chop shop, adulterated, and sold piece by piece.

The chop shop, a shadowy cavern underneath the Spruce Street Bridge, reeked of motor oil and cold hard cash. The proprietor, a man known by the name of Slim, was all smiles when the girls came through, his gold tooth glinting with the gleam of profit as he took in the newest offerings.

Life followed this pattern, until the fateful night they went out for what was to be "just another car." The night was quiet, the city's hum a distant lullaby as they approached their quarry: an opulent black SUV. It was a fortress of a vehicle, the tinted windows obscuring any view within or without. Quick and efficient as always, Jasmine jimmied the locks, Keira kept a lookout, Lola hot-wired the ignition, and Tia drove. They were a well-oiled machine, swift and silent.

But this wasn't just any SUV. It was the chariot of a kingpin, a man whose very name sparked fear in the hearts of those who whispered it: Don Moreno. A man who counted every dime, who knew the stitching of the leather seats as well as the murmur of secrets in his ranks.

The theft was seamless, the girls' confidence ballooning with their success. It was only when reports started scattering through the streets, whispers turning into outright warnings, that they realized their grave error. Don Moreno's fury scoured the city, his influence creeping into every corner, every shadowed alley, seeking his prized possession and ready to spill blood for its return.

Inside their shared apartment, panic brewed like a storm. Jasmine paced, her mind racing, while Keira checked and rechecked the locks. Lola tried to think of a plan, and Tia sat by the window, fear constricting her heart as she held their dog, Peekaboo, close.

Two days passed with no sign of the kingpin's wrath, but the girls knew it was the calm before the storm. On the third day, a sleek black car rolled up to their block, and two burly men got out, their eyes scanning the facades of the homes. The message was clear—Don Moreno knew someone here had taken his prized vehicle, and he would turn over the whole neighborhood to find it.

It wasn't just about them anymore. Their families, their neighborhood, their world was at risk. Something had to be done.

A plan began to hatch among whispered breaths and desperate glances. They couldn't go to the police—everyone knew Don Moreno had ears even within the force. No, it was up to them to undo their own tapestry of thievery.

They decided to return the SUV, to park it right where they had taken it from, with a note contained within that read: "A misunderstanding. Hope this clears it up." They cleaned it, wiped it free of fingerprints, and removed any trace that it had ever been anywhere but its rightful place.

Cloaked by midnight's embrace, the four girls drove the SUV back to its home. Their hearts banged against their ribs, their breath fogged the windows. Parking the car, they let it sit, a silent offering of peace, hoping it would appease the kingpin's wrath.

The next morning, news trickled down the vine: Don Moreno's SUV was back, no harm done, the seat warmer still set to his preference. Word on the street was, he was impressed by the audacity, enough so that he let the incident pass as a strange anomaly.

Jasmine, Keira, Lola, and Tia held their breath until the danger had evidently passed, the peace of their families secured. And as they promised each other they'd never again venture into the night's deadly allure, they watched Peekaboo dance around, oblivious to the chaos that had almost consumed them all. Newark breathed on, vigilant, as the girls' tale settled into the cracks of its streets, a tempest tamed, a lesson carved into the marrow of their souls.

Black in the Ghetto

By Bottega Boy Dee

Born where sirens sing us lullabies,
Under flickering lights and broken skies.
Where dreams get clipped like they wings too wide,
And hope walks slow 'cause too many died.
He Black—skin kissed by the sun too long,
But they see danger where they should see strong.
He walk with pride, but the world stay shook,
Treat him like a chapter they scared to look.
Corner store trips turn to close calls,
Police pass by like they hunting for flaws.
Mama pray hard that he make it home,
While he dodge more traps than a soldier alone.
The ghetto don't raise cowards, it breed steel,
Where love look tough and the pain feel real.
Ain't no silver spoons or white picket fence,
Just food stamps, hustle, and self-defense.
He seen brothers fall to the block or the pen,
He wonder if he'll ever feel peace again.
But he got that fire they can't destroy,
Even when life try to break that boy.
He a father, a son, a soul with depth,
A poet in silence, a voice they kept.
Don't label him lost, don't call him less—
He surviving a system designed to oppress.
But even in the chaos, he still rise,
A phoenix in chains with fearless eyes.
'Cause being Black in the ghetto ain't shame or sin—
It's proof that kings still breathe within.

Pawned by Monique Diaz

By Bottega Boy Dee

Monique Diaz, lost in the game,
Played motherhood like it came with no name.
Used her daughter like a piece on a board,
Just a pawn to push, never a child adored.
She smiled for the 'Gram, but behind closed doors,
She let love die and cracked open more.
No bedtime talks, no steady hand—
Just a phone in her face and demands on demand.
She swore she was solid, swore she did right,
But the mirror don't lie in the dead of night.
Parenting poor, truth hard to digest,
She failed every test, though she claimed she's the best.
The only man who stood through the storm,
Believed the child was his since she was born.
He gave all he had, time, money, and tears,
Only to be played after all those years.
She told him one day, cold as the snow:
"She ain't yours, just wanted your dough."
He stared in silence, crushed inside,
Still loved that child, though Monique lied.
Unprotected nights, chasing what's fast,
No roots, no future, just ghosts from her past.
Gold-digging ways with a bitter disguise,
Blaming the world while feeding it lies.
The court don't lie and the clock don't stall,
She's losing her rights, now she's losing it all.
Could've been a queen, a mother, a guide,
But she chose the hustle and let love slide.
This ain't just dirt, it's a lesson in truth,
About what we carry and what we lose.
A child ain't currency, a man ain't a bank,
And love don't live where there's selfish ranks.
So Monique, if you're listening, if this hits deep—
Understand seeds you plant are the ones you reap.
One day that daughter will ask you why,

And you'll have no answer but a silent cry.

One Night In Harlem With a Friend

Once an acclaimed heartbreaker, Marcus Barnes had roamed through his life as the ultimate player, gliding from one fleeting affair to the next with the expertise and allure that made him notorious. A life of lavish parties and passing romances was all he knew-until a brisk spring weekend in Harlem with his best friend,

Elijah Price, would set the stage for a story that would unfold into a tapestry of trust, betrayal, forgiveness, friendship, and hope...

Marcus and Elijah, a dynamic pair since their high school days, descended upon New York City for what was supposed to be a brief escape from their bustling lives in Atlanta. Both successful in their fields—Marcus in real estate and Elijah in law—they looked forward to enjoying the change of pace and the vibrant

Harlem culture, never suspecting that the trip would signal a monumental change in their lives.

It was a chance encounter at a jazz club on the heart of Malcolm X Boulevard, amidst the enthralling sounds of a saxophone wailing through the dizzying haze of music and low lights, that they met her. Laila Thompson, with her radiant smile and commanding presence, was a local artist whose work celebrated the rich history and diversity of her beloved Harlem.

Captivated by her passion and flair, both men felt an undeniable connection that neither had ever experienced before. Her laughter was a melody, and her words spun around them like an enchanting spell.

As Marcus and Elijah each sought to win Laila's affection, their attempts inadvertently exposed the seedier sides of their charm.

Marcus found himself entrapped in the very games he used to play, feeling a jealousy and desire that gripped him like never before.

Elijah, always the more introspective, began questioning his own motives and values, as he struggled to reconcile his burgeoning feelings with his lifelong friendship with Marcus..

Tensions soared as the long weekend drew to a close, coming to a head in a heated confrontation neither man was prepared for.

Accusations flew, and years of friendship threatened to unravel over the woman who had unexpectedly captured both their hearts. In a fit of rage over what seemed like a betrayal from his best friend, Marcus left, abandoning Elijah to his turmoil.

Back in Atlanta, the chasm between the two friends grew wider, laden with unspoken words and the weight of remorse. Marcus, wrestling with his playboy past, realized the profound impact Laila had made on him. He longed to seek her out, to prove to her—and to himself-that he was capable of real, lasting love.

Elijah, on the other hand, mired in guilt, chose to step back from the fray, giving up his pursuit and mourning the loss of both Laila and his friendship with Marcus.

It was through Laila's artistry, a poignant exhibit in Atlanta in which she depicted her journey through love and self-discovery, that reconciliation began. Her evocative works were an outpouring of the genuine connections she sought in life, untouched by games of the heart.

Touched deeply by the raw honesty of the paintings, Marcus found the courage to reach out to Elijah, laying bare his vulnerabilities and offering a sincere plea for forgiveness.

With Laila's art as a catalyst, Marcus and Elijah began to mend the tapestry of their friendship, reweaving the fibers of trust that had been frayed by jealousy and misunderstanding. And it was in this renewal that they each discovered the essence of love: not in the fervent rush of conquest, but in the quiet strength of genuine connection and unwavering support for one another.

Love, after all, was more than desire—it was the unyielding hope they shared, the friendship that endured, and the forgiveness that freed them from the past. And while the journey ahead was uncertain, Marcus, Elijah, and Laila moved forward, embracing the complexity of their entwined paths, under the watchful, vibrant skies of Harlem.

I Am Not Your Pawn

By BottegaBoyDee

You named me Aaliyah Faith Diaz...
but never taught me what faith really meant.
Used my name like a ticket,
like a pass to the rent.
Mama... nah, Monique.
'Cause you stopped being "Mom" the day you
chose men over me,
chose money over meals,
chose your feelings over how I feel.
You used my tears like receipts,
cashed my pain into courtrooms and pity.
Told every man I was his,
then laughed behind backs like it was a skit.
But I ain't no punchline.
I was a child... not a lifeline to your next dime.
You told the only man who stayed,
"I only used you for your pay."
He looked at me different that day.
Not because I was less,
but because you were.
And I saw the hurt behind his silence,
a man who gave love and got violence.
Mama, do you even see me?
Or just the check with my name on it?
Do you remember my birthdays?
Or just who you argued with before cake?
You lay up with strangers,
while I lay awake wondering if you'll come back.
Your parenting? Piss poor,
but your pride is too loud to hear the facts.
The judge doesn't see a mother anymore.
Even your own lawyer went out the door.

The system ain't perfect—but it noticed
you ain't tried.
You ain't healed.
You ain't even apologized.
I'm not your pawn.
I'm not your come-up.
I'm not your second chance
to clean your mess up.
You gave me a name that means faith,
but never gave me a reason to believe in you.
And now... I don't.
And I won't.
Because I deserve peace.
I deserve the truth.
And one day, when I'm grown,
I'll break every chain that ever tied me to you.
I am Aaliyah Faith Diaz.
And you don't get to wear that with pride.
You lost that right
the moment you lied.

I'm not cocky I'm confident

BottegaBoy Dee

They call me cocky, but they misunderstand,
I don't boast with empty words, or wave a heavy hand.
I walk with my chest up, my spirit held high,
Not to belittle, but to reach for the sky.
Cocky is loud, needing others to see,
Confident is quiet, it lives deep in me.
I don't need to step on someone to shine,
My growth, my grind — that glow is mine.
I've stumbled, I've fallen, I've learned from the pain,
That's why I stand stronger, not chasing fame.
Cocky is shallow, it feeds on applause,
Confidence is steady, it knows its own cause.
So don't twist my silence, don't misread my stance,
This is not arrogance, just self-made chance.
I'm not above you, I'm just true to my core,
Cocky takes, but confidence builds more.

When the Cards Went Silent"

The morning came, but screens stayed dim,
No balance shown, no hopeful hymn.
A mother sighed, her cart stood still,
Dreams paused between the bread and milk.
The hum of checkout lines grew tense,
Whispers carried common sense:
"System's down," they softly said,
But hearts heard louder fears instead.
For years, that card had held the weight,
Of families' meals, of struggle's fate.
A piece of plastic, small yet grand,
A lifeline resting in tired hands.
Now silence filled the grocery air,
A quiet cry of public care.
Not just hunger in the aisles that day,
But faith and hope both swept away.
Still — people helped where systems failed,
Shared what little they had, unscaled.
For when the cards could speak no more,
Kindness opened every store.

EBT Gone Silent

They woke up early, same ol' grind,
Swipe the card, pray it still decline?
Nah — this time it's deeper than that,
Whole system froze, can't feed the pack.
Mama in line with a baby cryin',
Cashier shrug, "System's down, I'm tryin'."
Groceries sittin', hearts start sinkin',
World don't stop, but man — it's thinkin'.
That lil' blue card been keepin' lights on,
Late-night meals, survival strong.
Now the screen just blinkin' blank,
No word, no code, no food, no rank.
They call it "temporary," same old song,
But hunger don't wait, it don't take long.
You see, when the gov shut the lifeline tight,
The people still found a way to fight.
Neighbors shared plates, split what they had,
Old heads nodded, "Yeah, it's bad."
But faith ain't plastic, hope don't bend,
We still gon' make it — that's how we end.

The unmasking

In sheep's attire, the wolf parades, a masquerade of shallow charades.

With smiling masks, they draw you near, Feigning friendship, insincere.

In the light of day, they clasp your hand, promising to be there, to understand.

But shadows whisper truths untold, Of a heart that's callous, cruel, and cold.

With honeyed words, they weave a net, a trap of trust that's soon to set.

You share the depths of your secret seas, Not seeing the forest for the trees.

But time, the teller of hidden tales, Unveils the mask as friendship fails.

The knife of betrayal, sharp and sleek, Strikes in silence, wounds so deep.

Like autumn leaves, their colors change,
The hues of loyalty rearrange.

A friend who's foe, a guise so thin, Reveals the adversary within.

Yet in this dance of duplicity, Emerges a truth that sets us free.

For real friends, pure, like stars that glow, Shine brighter still next to a foe.

Different Streets, Same Heart

Bottega Boy Dee

He's Harlem-born—raised where the struggle stays loud,
Dreams climb fire escapes, reaching through the crowd.
Project walls whispered lessons, nights cold, eyes wide,
He learned young that peace don't live where pain hides.
She's from Pennsylvania, where the houses stand proud,
Quiet streets, open skies, no need for a crowd.
Her world was calm, safe, untouched by the fight,
Never knew what it meant to pray through the night.
He's seen things she can't picture—tears on cracked floors,
Friends lost too early, dreams locked behind doors.
She's known comfort, the warmth of steady hands,
Never had to run before she could stand.
Yet when they met—it was soul recognizing soul,
Two halves of a story finally made whole.

She saw past his scars, the truth in his eyes,
He saw in her a softness the world rarely supplies.
She taught him that love could be gentle, not pain,
That sunlight can grow even after the rain.
He showed her that life isn't perfect or neat,
That strength is surviving with heart still beating.
Now they build something between their two worlds,
A Harlem boy, a Pennsylvania girl.
Different beginnings, but the same heart inside—
Love don't ask where you're from—it just wants to ride

The cost of kinship

Upon a gleaming metal steed, The man bestowed on son a deed:

'To ride with caution, tame the speed, To safer grounds, your path do lead."

This trust was bound in chrome and leather, A pact 'twixt storm and calming weather.

The bike, it roared—a beast uncaged, With freedom's tune, the boy engaged.

Through streets that call with whispering danger, To destinations of no stranger, He ventured forth, as bidden fair,

To realms where tires kiss air with care..

Yet fate, a cruel and twisted author, Penned a chapter wrought with slaughter;

The son, embroiled in metal's clash, His steed reduced to dust and ash.

The phone rang out, a siren's wail, The mother's words did then unveil The havoc written on that day,

As rubber scars the asphalt's fray.

The father's heart, though struck with dread,

Raised no ire, but calm instead

"Stand tall," he urged, "bear consequence,

To err is human; recompense."

The son agreed, with solemn vow, To mend the wreckage, toil, and plough.

Yet time did pass, the debt stood tall, No coin returned, no effort to appall.
The father's patience, now threadbare, Sought earnestly for reparation fair.
But mother's will was lacking force,
No urging made to take recourse.
Oh, what sorrow in this tale,
Where promises like old ship's sail, Were left to rot, untouched, ignored,
While the debt remained, the burden stored.
For in this dance between the three, An honor's price weighed heavily.
Responsibility, a chain,
That bound the son in tacit pain.
A lesson hard, a fissure deep, The motorcycle, now a heap,
Spoke of a trust that's maimed and scarred, When words are wind, and actions marred.
Thus ends the verse, though tales ring true, That trust once broken, is hard to renew,
And debts unpaid, yield heavy cost, In respect and love, tragically

Lesson in the SHU

Bottega Boy Dee

He was a man built from calloused hands,
A provider, a dreamer with solid plans.
A family man who worked each day,
Till a bike crash took that grind away
Laid up, broke down, the bills came due,
So when a call for security came through,
He said, "God, this might be my break,"
A short-term gig — the risk he'd take.
But the plan went left, like fate gone wild,
A bag chased hard turned self on trial.
Iron bars replaced his open sky,
His freedom traded for cold steel nights.
Inside the walls, the rules were clear —
Walk the yard bold, or drown in fear.
"Paperwork solid," they said, "or fold,"
Proof of truth was your shield of gold.
He told his fiancée, "It's how things go,
You don't get it, but in here we know."
But she brushed it off — love grown thin,
Her heart out there, his locked within.
The papers never came, the doubts took root,
They shipped him off — SHU boots and suit.
Six long months in that concrete tomb,
Where silence screams and minds consume.
He battled demons no one could see,
Verbal wars, lost sanity.
Each letter he wrote, poured soul and bone,
"Baby, please, just bring me home."
But her ink slowed, her tone turned stern,
Said, "I'm teaching you a lesson — you'll learn."
Little did she know behind that door,
He was learning more than ever before.

He learned who stands when the lights go dim,
Who truly rides — and who just swims.
He learned that love can fade like air,
And pain don't heal just 'cause you care.
So when that six months came and passed,
He walked out changed — not built to last
For games or pity, or half-love schemes,
He'd buried that man inside his dreams.
Now he moves silent, wise, and cold,
With a story heavy, hard, and bold.
From a crash, to a cell, to a soul renewed —
He learned his lesson — just not the one she knew.

Bottega Boy Dee

Name ring bells — Big Dee, but they call him Bottega Boy Dee,
Resourceful by nature, born to grind and succeed.
Didn't wait on a chance, he built his own lane,
Turned vision into value, turned hustle into name.
Came from the soil where the hungry don't sleep,
Where dreams cost time, and talk ain't cheap.
But Dee had drive — sharper than glass,
Knew how to turn struggle into champagne and class.
Then he linked with a team, brothers cut from the same cloth,
The Bottega Boys, all shining, no loss.
Ambassadors of bubbles, gold bottles and grace,
Turning every celebration into a power embrace.
They toast to success, not luck or a trend,
But the nights they ain't quit, and the rules they bend.
Each pop of that cork, another milestone won,
Another chapter written, another dream begun.
Now when you see them step through, suits tailored tight,
Gold in their hands, confidence in sight.
They don't just sip — they symbolize reign,

Turning pain into polish, struggle into champagne.
And at the head of that toast, you already see,
The heart of the hustle — Bottega Boy Dee.
From the block to the boardroom, his story's proof —
You can rise with class and still stand on truth.

Two Walks, One Road

He came from Harlem, where the sirens sang at night,
Streetlights flickered stories, some wrong, some right.
Raised in the projects, concrete dreams beneath his feet,
Every block a battlefield, survival bittersweet.
She grew up in Pennsylvania, where the lawns stayed green,
Porch swings whispered softly, life calm and serene.
A world of quiet mornings, skies painted wide and blue,
Her storms were gentle showers—his skies rarely knew.
He's seen the struggle, the pain, the fight to stay alive,
Learned early that love don't bloom where you barely survive.
She's seen comfort, safety wrapped in her days,
Never had to hustle just to find her way.
When they met, it was lightning—worlds colliding in flame,
Two souls from two stories, yet their hearts beat the same.
He spoke in rhythm, in truth, in lessons hard-earned,
She listened and felt something new, something learned.
He taught her that peace ain't a place, it's a fight,
That stars shine brighter when born from the night.
She showed him that calm doesn't mean you're weak,
That love can be quiet and still run deep.
Now they walk together, though from different lands,
One reaching for hope, the other holding his hands.
Two lives, two worlds, the past they can't hide—
But love don't care where you're from, only what's inside.

Love at first sight

Upon a digital thread we met, 'twas p.o.f that cast the net, A platform of romantic quests, where hearts beat fast in hopeful chests.

When first we spoke, the screen alight, I saw in you my endless night, Your icy blue eyes pierced the veil, my heart set sail, love's hallowed grail.

Fresh from the shadows, life's hard joint, I stood, a soul at freedom's point.

Yet in you saw I something true, A kindred flame, a start anew.

We ventured to the park so green, A picnic spread, a tranquil scene,

There whispered you with words so fine,

"We'll be each other's spine."

You laid bare your soul, promised to hold, Through thick and thin, through heat, through cold.

Our hands entwined like roots of oak, In each other's strength, we never broke.

Remember, my love, I am the shield, Together, a team, we take the field.

Through every storm we shall not sway, For I am yours, through night, through day.

Your steadfast promise, a beacon bright, In our shared journey through the night.

In you, I found my heart's own twin, Together, a formidable skin.

We are the balm for winter's bite, And in our union, we find light.

So know, my love, I'm ever near, Through every laugh, through each tear.

Bound by the vows not spoken but felt, Before the fates our hearts did melt.

In every challenge, our love's song, Together, my dear, we are strong.

To The Virgin Mary

In the heart of the bustling city, there lived a young woman named Mary. She was a modern-day incarnation of purity and kindness, a beacon of hope in a world that often felt devoid of it. She worked at a non-profit organization dedicated to helping the less fortunate, and her gentle spirit and tireless devotion to her work made her beloved by all who knew her.

Despite the bustle and technological hum that surrounded her, Mary maintained a simple lifestyle. She favored modest attire, and while many her age were lost in the flow of social media and the quest for material success, Mary found her joy in the tranquility of her community garden and the warm smiles she exchanged with strangers.

Mary's apartment was sparsely decorated, with sunlight pouring in through the windows, illuminating her collection of well-tended potted plants. On her bedside table lay a modern adaptation of the Bible, its passages marked by colorful tabs and annotations penned in her flowing cursive.

The city was ripe with tales of this enigmatic figure, a woman untouched by cynicism or despair. They spoke of her volunteer work, her days spent serving meals to the homeless or teaching underprivileged children to read and write. Mary's presence was a rumor of serenity, a whisper of something ancient and incorruptible vested in the fabric of contemporary chaos.

One day, as she walked through the city square, a dove alighted on her shoulder, a momentary hush fell upon the throng of people. For an instant, time seemed to stand still. Citizens who were locked in their routines glanced up from their phones and paperwork, caught by the peculiarity of the scene. There was Mary, unfazed by the sudden attention, whispering to the bird as if an old friend had come to call.

As the bird took flight, an idea sparked in Mary's heart. She started gathering people from the community to join her in a new movement—a movement of compassion and unity. It was as if she were sowing seeds of purity and love across the concrete jungle, transforming it into a garden where human connection could flourish once more.

One evening, during a community meeting held in the park, the group sat encircled under the stars, speaking earnestly about their dreams for a kinder society. As Mary shared her vision, a soft glow seemed to radiate from her, not unlike the aura depicted in ancient paintings. There, in the sprawling urbanity, it was as if the Virgin Mary from centuries past had been reborn, her spirit of nurturing and peace profound and relevant amidst the city's steel frames and pulsing lights.

Her story became one of legend, not because she performed miracles or bore an immaculate conception, but because she lived with a timeless grace, inspiring those around her to rekindle their own sparks of benevolence and goodwill. Mary was a symbol of what the human heart could achieve when it chose to remain untainted by the shadows of the age.

In this modern world dominated by fleeting trends and relentless ambition, the Virgin Mary of our story stood out as a reminder that some qualities are eternal. Love, care, and a belief in the good of humanity—these were the miracles she spread, these were the virtues she nurtured, rooting them deeply in the soul of the modern age, where they were needed the most.

The Weight of a Name

Once there was a man named Michael who made a mistake that cost him his freedom. Despite the harsh reality of his incarceration, his wife, Angela, remained his steadfast beacon of support. Literally standing by his side through the thick bars and the impenetrable walls, Angela visited him every week for five long months. Her love and loyalty were the life raft keeping Michael afloat in the turbulent sea that was jail life.

As Michael's release date approached, he dreamed of returning home - to be the man Angela deserved and to become a positive influence in his community. Little did he know, an unexpected tempest was brewing that would test his resolve even further.

During those months of unwavering support, Angela's loneliness had led to an ill-fated liaison with an officer at the jail, Officer Daniels, a man with his own set of twisted ideals. Consumed by the forbidden flame of their secret romance, she found herself lost in the moment. But once the affair came to light, Daniels coldly turned his back on her, revealing his true nature. Worse still, he and his colleagues began treating Angela with contempt and malice.

When Michael walked free at last, the air he breathed felt thick with possibilities.. The streets welcomed him back, and the glares of days past were replaced with nods of respect. He was set on turning his life's lessons into a public testament, to inspire the youth in his hood to choose a different path.

However, the past has a way of echoing into the present, and the whispers of Angela's indiscretions soon reached Michael's ears. The hurt was unimaginable, but his response was not what anyone anticipated. Rather than revert to his old ways, Michael turned to the pen, hoping to find solace and redemption through writing his life story.

But this tale isn't one without its villains. Officer Daniels, along with his corrupt colleagues, learned of Michael's intentions to publish his memoirs, a project that was sure to bring not just local fame, but also substantial financial gain. Their greedy eyes saw an opportunity for blackmail as they threatened to unveil Angela's indiscretions unless Michael paid a steep price. They even went as far as to target his mother and son, aiming to strike where it hurt most to ensure their silence.

Faced with these threats, Michael stood at a crossroad. Surrender to the blackmail and protect his family's peace or expose the officers and risk the wrath that may follow. In the darkness that surrounded him, Michael found his answer in the strength that got him through his time in jail. He decided to confront his past with integrity and the honesty that shaped his newfound

Fighting against the corruption with both the power of his story and the law, Michael sought justice. His journey was not just about clearing his name or creating a legacy; it was about reclaiming his life and standing tall for those who felt voiceless. For Angela, the mistakes were immense, but they led her to a path of seeking redemption and learning to forgive herself. And for Michael, the tale of his life, with all its twists and turmoils, became a message of transformation and courage, a beacon for anyone striving to rise above their darkest hours.

A diamond in the street

In the heart of Philadelphia's grittiest ghettos, where decayed buildings loomed over trash-laden streets like tired guardians of despair, a woman known only as Diamond shaped her existence. She wasn't born into luxury, nor did she embrace the common life of hard work and silent suffering that many around her bore like a cross. Diamond's dreams glittered with the same sharpness as her name, and her aspirations soared way above the squalor that surrounded her.

Diamond walked with the confidence of someone who knew the power of her beauty. She was a vixen, a seductress, the siren of Philly's underbelly. But behind her enchanting smile was an ice-cold strategy. She didn't want love, she didn't yearn for a quiet life with a white picket fence. Diamond sought power, and she knew exactly where to find it.

In this concrete jungle, the sound of gunfire was more common than that of wedding bells, and the reigning princes were the ballers, the kingpins, and the up-and-coming drug dealers. These were the men Diamond hunted—her prey, lined in pockets heavy with dirty cash and ephemeral authority.

With a team as ruthless as her ambition, Diamond devised a deadly dance. They called her crew "The Silencers." They worked with the precision of seasoned assassins: seduce, deceive, and eliminate. With every conquest, she and her team would rob these dealers blind, stripping them of money, drugs, and, if necessary, life. Their motto? Leave no witness.

For months, Diamond's deadly waltz went unchallenged. The streets whispered her tales, and she became a phantom—a legend that draped over Philly like a chilling mist. But every action yields a consequence, and bloodshed begets bloodshed.

Among the survivors and the paranoid, an alliance formed of those who had lost much and sought vengeance..

These dealers weren't just street-savvy; they were war-torn soldiers who thrived in the face of adversity. They had clawed their way up from the very gutters that now ran with the blood of their fallen comrades. United by loss and the primal desire for survival, they called themselves "The Seekers."

The city transformed into a battlefield, the gangs moved not just for control but survival. The Seekers and The Silencers became the heartbeats of a war-zone, their conflicts laying waste to street corners and turning homes into hideouts and fortresses. The dark whispers in the ghettos had hushes of betrayal, tight-lipped informants, and sudden violence.

Diamond realized too late that the game had changed. The hunters had become the hunted, and her notoriety now painted her as a prime target rather than an enigmatic ghost. It became harder to move in the shadows when every shadow could be a potential enemy.

The war climaxed one fateful night when the moon, a cold witness to the city's sins, cast its pale light on streets littered with casualties of the war. The Silencers, cornered and outgunned, with Diamond in the eye of the storm, fought not for wealth or reputation, but simply for the chance to see another sunrise.

When the dust settled and the acrid smell of gunpowder seeped into the cracks of what remained, Diamond lay wounded amongst the ruins of her shattered dreams. As she looked upon the broken bodies and the shattered lives left in her wake, she wondered if her thirst for power was worth the lives it had cost.

And so, the tale of Diamond's reign ended as abruptly as it began, a stark warning that in the ruthless streets of Philly, the crown is heavy, and often the head that wears it lies uneasy—and sometimes, severed.

Lessons from the Lost

the heart of Westridge, a place that mirrored the struggles of urban life, stood a teenager, just a silhouette against the harsh backdrop of the city's never-ending clamor. Jackson, known to many as "Jax," was a name that resonated with trouble. His reputation preceded him down the graffiti-stained alleyways and across the smog-laden skies—the kid was into every crime there was to offer: theft, vandalism, barroom brawls, you name it.

Jax's life had been a cacophony of wailing sirens and whispered warnings since he was old enough to ride a bike. There had been no guiding hand to steer him off his path, no familial compass to guide him home. His mother had walked out on the family when he was just seven, and his father was a ghost lost to the bottle, offering nothing but empty promises and lingering resentment.

The streets became Jax's tutor, each illicit deed a lesson in survival. He ran with a crew that thrived on chaos, brothers and sisters in shadows who looked out for each other because no one else would. It was an unspoken rule they all lived by-trust only those who've got as much to lose as you.

But fate, it seemed, had other plans for the wayward son of Westridge. It came in the devastating blow of a sledgehammer, crushing all the foundations of Jax's fragile reality. The crew had been ambushed mid-heist, the plan leaking to the cops like a decomposing secret. Jax had escaped in the chaos, but the cost was dire.

Amid the angry glow of flashing red and blue, Jax's world fractured at the news that his closest cremates, Miles and Tasha, hadn't made it out. They paid the price for their hubris, young lives snatched by a storm of bullets in the darkness of a botched robbery.

Guilt hounded Jax like a shadow, each step a reminder of the ones his friends could no longer take. In isolation, haunted by the ghosts of his choices, Jax wrestled with despair. And it was in that wrestling—a sweat-soaked, tear-stained struggle—that he grappled with something deeper.

Grief became a crucible, and in that molten agony, Jax began to hear the whispers of something greater than the tinny echo of his own desolation. It was an unshakable sense that in the core of his being, there was more to his life than the crime-riddled pages of his past.

They said that sometimes, God moves in mysterious ways, through loss and pain, a calling in the wilderness of sorrow. Jax felt that presence, an undeniably powerful force that seemed to compel him towards a sliver of light in his darkened world.

After months of evading the law, reality finally caught up with him. One chilly dawn, as the first blush of sunrise painted the sky in hues of hope, Jax found himself surrounded by the inevitability of steel handcuffs and the solemn faces of officers who, in another life, might've been his guardians instead of his captors.

The trial was swift—a parade of evidence and witnesses that painted Jax as the poster child for lost causes. Yet, amidst the deluge of his wrongdoings, something had shifted within Jax. In the silence of his cell, he began to peel back the layers of his anger and disillusionment

. The cold, hard bench of the holding cell was his altar, the sterile, artificial lights his stained-glass windows. He prayed not for absolution but for the strength to face the consequences of his actions and the opportunity to atone and rebuild a life scattered into disarray..

Youth detention was harsh, but it was also where Jax found unlikely salvation. He encountered volunteers who believed in rehabilitation over retribution, educators who saw past his rap sheet to the potential beneath. Slowly, the teen who was initiated into crime before adulthood learned about redemption and the power of change.

Years passed, marked by the incremental victories of a troubled youth clawing his way up from the depths. When he emerged from the confines of correctional education, something remarkable had transpired. Jax, with a GED in hand and a new purpose etched in his heart, was no longer defined by his dark past but illuminated by the grace of a second chance.

While no path to redemption is without its brambles and setbacks, Jax dedicated himself to working with at-risk youth, repurposing his cautionary tale as a lighthouse for those adrift in similar storms. His was a testimony of transformation—proof that even in our darkest moments, there are melodies of hope whispered by a calling that redeems, restores, and ultimately

The fathers fight

Once there lived a father named Marcus, whose world revolved around his two young children, Ava and Ethan. Their laughter was the music he danced to, and their smiles were the light guiding him through the darkest tunnels. But life, as often it does, took a sharp turn when Marcus's partner fell into a web of misdeeds, tearing the family apart.

Amidst the chaos of accusations and misunderstandings, the children were taken from Marcus, leaving his heart shattered in the corridors of the family court system. Days blended into nights as he fought for the right to hold his children once more, each court session an echo of desperation in the hollows of justice.

The situation grew heavier with every passing moment, as Marcus's own mother-in-law, fueled by bitter emotions, vowed with venomous words, "If I have anything to do with it, you will not see your kids until they're 18 years of age." Her decree settled like a stone in Marcus's stomach, anchoring him to his worst fears.

Years staggered by, each day a reminder of the echoing absence in his home. The walls that once echoed with joyful giggles now stood silent, a testament to his loss. Marcus, battling waves of stress and depression, saw his hopes waning with the setting sun.

Yet inside him, a spark refused to die—a father's love that no court could extinguish. One day, as the years of separation bore heavily upon him, Marcus turned to social media, the modern-day scroll of life's happenings, with a flicker of hope in his heart.

His fingers danced with trepidation over the keyboard as he typed his daughter's name into the search bars of Facebook and Instagram.

Miraculously, fate smiled upon him that day. As if guided by a higher force, Marcus stumbled upon Ava's profile. Tears blurred his vision as he scrolled through her life, digitally pieced together through pictures and posts.

With a trembling heart, he reached out, crafting a message with all the love and pain of a father kept away. When Ava replied, a connection long severed began to mend, stitch by digital stitch.. Marcus shared stories and photographs, snippets of memories and silent cheers for her accomplishments unseen.

Ava, grown yet still his little girl, saw sincerity and love in his words. She invited him to her track meet, an olive branch extended across the chasm of years. Marcus, with a spirit lighter than it had been in a decade, joined the crowd at the sidelines as Ava raced, a fierce comet streaking down the track. With every step she took, a piece of his broken heart healed.

Time continued its inexorable march, and Ava donned her cap and gown, her high school years a chapter closing with a swift turn of the tassel. Marcus, now a constant presence, beamed with pride on graduation day. College beckoned, a new journey for Ava, and he was there to support her every step of the way.

The story of Marcus and his children is one of resilience, a reminder that the bonds of love can endure even the harshest storms life throws our way. Through his tenacity and undying hope, a father, once severed from his most precious gifts, found his way back to them, proving that sometimes, even the most painful journeys can lead to beautiful destinations.

The Devotion of Amara

In a quaint and sleepy village nestled between rolling hills and serene rivers, there was a girl named Amara. She was known for her compassion, her deep faith, and the gentle way she carried herself through life's trials. Her heart was like a beacon, steadfast in the belief that despite the chaos around, goodness would prevail because she held onto the promises written in the old pages of her well-worn Bible.

Amara grew up listening to the stories of old, the tales of prophets and the whispers of revelations. She was taught that there would be signs-signs that would herald the end of times, and the return of the Divine. Among these signs were the sounds of the celestial horns, a call that would resonate through the very core of existence.

One day, as the sun dipped below the horizon, casting a golden glow over the land, the air was split by the sound of the horns.

It was not a sound that was heard with the ears; it was deeper, more profound—felt in the marrow of one's bones. Amara, who was tending to her family's humble garden, stood still, her hands pausing mid-air as she recognized the herald. The horns spoke of the last days, just as it was written.

Around her, the world seemed oblivious to the call, but Amara, with her heart laid open to the divine truths, knew what this meant. Over the years, she had often wondered if she was naive to believe so fervently in promises from ancient texts.. But now, with each horn's cry, her belief was vindicated—God was keeping His promise.

Days passed, and the people who had heard the call noticed a change. There was a lightness to their being, an unspoken understanding that rippled through their community. Though it was never spoken aloud, they collectively knew their conviction was about to be rewarded.

Then, one radiant morning, as the first rays of the dawn pierced through the gentle mist, the sky unfolded in a spectacle of celestial glory. Brilliant beams of light cascaded to Earth, and within them, beings of pure light descended.

These were the angels spoken of in sacred scripture, their presence overwhelming in its love and authority.

Amara watched, her heart full, as the beings of light touched down upon the earth. She noticed that they only approached those who had heard the call, who had lived by the compassion and hope that was central to their faith. They were the believers, and now, they were to be taken to the divine embrace promised to them.

Those who had turned a deaf ear to the sounds of faith and love, who had lived ensnared by their disbelief or apathy, remained untouched by the angels. They stood rooted to the spot, witnesses to a truth they had denied, now coming to pass before their eyes.. There was no malice in their leaving behind-merely a testament to the choices made in the life they led.

Amara, along with the others, felt the touch of the angels as warmth that bathed her spirit. Looking to the sky, she knew it was time to leave this earthly realm behind. As she ascended, a profound peace enveloped her—a peace that whispered of the start of an eternal journey in the presence of the divine, a journey promised to all who had kept faith.

And although the world below carried on, for those who ascended, it was the beginning of an existence where every whispered promise of the divine was fulfilled. In that moment of rapture, Amara remembered the words that had been etched into her soul, a message of everlasting love and salvation. For her, and for all like her, God had kept His promise.

One Night In Harlem With a Friend

Once an acclaimed heartbreaker, Marcus Barnes had roamed through his life as the ultimate player, gliding from one fleeting affair to the next with the expertise and allure that made him notorious. A life of lavish parties and passing romances was all he knew-until a brisk spring weekend in Harlem with his best friend,

Elijah Price, would set the stage for a story that would unfold into a tapestry of trust, betrayal, forgiveness, friendship, and hope...

Marcus and Elijah, a dynamic pair since their high school days, descended upon New York City for what was supposed to be a brief escape from their bustling lives in Atlanta. Both successful in their fields—Marcus in real estate and Elijah in law—they looked forward to enjoying the change of pace and the vibrant

Harlem culture, never suspecting that the trip would signal a monumental change in their lives.

It was a chance encounter at a jazz club on the heart of Malcolm X Boulevard, amidst the enthralling sounds of a saxophone wailing through the dizzying haze of music and low lights, that they met her. Laila Thompson, with her radiant smile and commanding presence, was a local artist whose work celebrated the rich history and diversity of her beloved Harlem.

Captivated by her passion and flair, both men felt an undeniable connection that neither had ever experienced before. Her laughter was a melody, and her words spun around them like an enchanting spell.

As Marcus and Elijah each sought to win Laila's affection, their attempts inadvertently exposed the seedier sides of their charm.

Marcus found himself entrapped in the very games he used to play, feeling a jealousy and desire that gripped him like never before.

Elijah, always the more introspective, began questioning his own motives and values, as he struggled to reconcile his burgeoning feelings with his lifelong friendship with Marcus..

Tensions soared as the long weekend drew to a close, coming to a head in a heated confrontation neither man was prepared for.

Accusations flew, and years of friendship threatened to unravel over the woman who had unexpectedly captured both their hearts. In a fit of rage over what seemed like a betrayal from his best friend, Marcus left, abandoning Elijah to his turmoil.

Back in Atlanta, the chasm between the two friends grew wider, laden with unspoken words and the weight of remorse. Marcus, wrestling with his playboy past, realized the profound impact Laila had made on him. He longed to seek her out, to prove to her—and to himself-that he was capable of real, lasting love.

Elijah, on the other hand, mired in guilt, chose to step back from the fray, giving up his pursuit and mourning the loss of both Laila and his friendship with Marcus.

It was through Laila's artistry, a poignant exhibit in Atlanta in which she depicted her journey through love and self-discovery, that reconciliation began. Her evocative works were an outpouring of the genuine connections she sought in life, untouched by games of the heart.

Touched deeply by the raw honesty of the paintings, Marcus found the courage to reach out to Elijah, laying bare his vulnerabilities and offering a sincere plea for forgiveness.

With Laila's art as a catalyst, Marcus and Elijah began to mend the tapestry of their friendship, reweaving the fibers of trust that had been frayed by jealousy and misunderstanding. And it was in this renewal that they each discovered the essence of love: not in the fervent rush of conquest, but in the quiet strength of genuine connection and unwavering support for one another.

Love, after all, was more than desire—it was the unyielding hope they shared, the friendship that endured, and the forgiveness that freed them from the past. And while the journey ahead was uncertain, Marcus, Elijah, and Laila moved forward, embracing the complexity of their entwined paths, under the watchful, vibrant skies of Harlem.

The view from with in

In corridors of echoed clink and clatter,

Behind the bars where shadows play and scatter, There waits a heart, with hopeful eyes so bright, For promised footsteps that would bring the light..

A solemn pact, etched deep within the mind, A balm to soothe the endless hours unkind.

The calendar's crossed days, a silent shout, For surely they, the loved, will seek him out.

Visitor's chair, an island in the grey, A stage for scenes of reunion's tender play.

The clock, a drum, ticks rhythms of false cheer, To paint a portrait of someone drawing near.

But silence weaves its web through sterile space, The chair remains untouched, an empty place.

The heavy air grows thick with phantom sounds, Of joyous laughter, heartbeats that resound.

Weeks string along like pearls on fraying thread, The rote routine, a dance with hope undead.

Each morning brings a resurgence of belief, Each nightfall sees the ghost of latent grief.

No tap upon the glass, no warming smile, No hands to press against the cold, stark tile.

The waiting game, played out on borrowed time,

A cruel charade, a hill too steep to climb.

Desire for closeness wraps in crushing hold, While memories, like dust, grow faint and old.

The jailbird longs for just a fleeting glance, To anchor him amidst his circumstance.

And yet no form emerges from the mist, No name is called, no presence on the list.

Abandonment, a shroud that cloaks the day, For promised steps that never came to sway.

The truth, a pill too bitter to digest, Brun bridges fade, put finally to rest.

In visage of an ever-empty guest, The soul concedes, with weary heart oppressed.

Hope flickers, dims, within the warden's care, Of whispered copes and frigid prison air.

He learns in time, what many have come to Promises, like dreams, don't always come true.

Another woman trash another woman Treasure

Once upon a time in the vibrant, bustling streets of Harlem, there was a young couple, Malik and Tiana, who were known for their fiery passion and equally heated arguments. They had been together long enough to know each other's triggers, yet on one sweltering summer's day, something unusual happened.

As they walked down the crowded sidewalk, dodging street performers and vendors, Tiana teased Malik with a flirtatious glint in her eyes, "Imma go see my new boo." It was the kind of joke she had made a hundred times before, but that day, Malik's pride was feeling

particularly fragile.

Eyes narrowed, Malik took the comment as a slight, believing respect was paramount and

Tiana had crossed a line. "Fine," he spat, his voice sharp as he pulled out his phone.

Within minutes, he dialed Nadia, Tiana's best friend, requesting her company under the pretext of needing advice. It was a rash decision driven by his need to one-up Tiana, to show that he could be just as teasingly cruel. Tiana stormed off, and Malik inserted an earbud, losing himself in the cacophony of Harlem's heartbeat, trying to cool down.

Later, as Nadia pushed open the door to Malik's cluttered apartment, she found him sipping a lukewarm beer on the sofa, tracks from Nas softly playing in the background.. Brooding turned into bantering, and the sun fell beyond the horizon as they navigated the delicate topic of his crumbling relationship.

It wasn't long before they were sharing secrets and recounting old stories, snickering at mishaps from past nights out. It was then, amid the laughter and the vulnerability, that their proximity drew them together in a way neither had anticipated.

As if by magnetic pull, their one moment of shared comfort morphed into many moments of passion sprawled across Malik's living room floor. They traversed from the balcony door to the brick fireplace on the opposite end, leaving no pillow unturned, no shadow untouched by their fervor. In the aftermath, as they lay catching their breath, Malik teased, "You're like a mop, moving all over the place."

What began as a quip became a nickname, a private joke that bonded them in a way neither could quite grasp at the time.

Months rolled by, taking Malik's affinity for New York with them. Looking for a fresh start, he relocated to another state, leaving memories and lingering what-ifs behind.

He found a new rhythm, a new life, and eventually, a new love. Yet there was something unspoken, a flicker of the past that danced just beyond reach—until, by some twist of fate, he bumped into Nadia during a surprise visit back in Harlem.

They hadn't spoken since that night, yet the moment they locked eyes, it was clear the ember of their connection had survived the winter of their absence. Conversation flowed as if the months apart were merely seconds, and laughter peeled away the layers of time and change.

Underneath it all, the fire they had was never extinguished... It simmered quietly, biding its time until they could acknowledge that what happened on the floor of Malik's old Harlem apartment was more than just shared warmth—it was a beginning waiting to be reignited.

Between The Lock & The Heart

In the grays and blues of penitentiary life, Donovan, whose worn features belied a softness seldom found along the rows of hardened faces, had been counting the sunsets for more years than he cared to remember. Each day carried the same monotonous rhythm, set against the backdrop of clanging bars and distant dreams.

Among the staff, there was one Correctional Officer (CO) who stood out like a rose amidst thorns—Officer Isabella Garcia. To Donovan, she wasn't just a CO; she was the embodiment of everything pure and beautiful that he had missed out on. Her peers often threw envious glances her way, treating her with a biting disdain they didn't bother to hide.

Donovan kept to himself, sketching fragments of hope in a worn notebook, a silent rebellion against the institution that bound him. Whenever Officer Garcia passed by, he would offer a respectful nod, a gesture she returned with a rare, authentic smile.

Their exchanges were minimal, limited to the confines of protocol. However, as time trickled by, Donovan found himself entranced by this woman, who treated her job with professionalism yet managed to retain a spark of kindness. He yearned to share his world with her, to offer her a glimpse into the poetry etched in each line of his sketches.

The trouble was that Donovan's intentions didn't go unnoticed by a group of inmates—old-timers like himself, who seemed to find pleasure in ensuring that no one else caught a break. They kept eyes on him like buzzards circling, ready to swoop in with taunts or interference should an opportunity to express his admiration arise.

But fate, it seemed, had its own designs. One sweltering summer day, as the basketball court throbbed with energy and rowdy shouts, Officer Garcia summoned Donovan to the staff office with a silent gesture. His guard up, ready for a reprimand or a random search, Donovan entered the cool, florescent-lit space.

Garcia closed the door behind them. The click of the lock was a soft sound that carried the weight of the world. Her eyes found his, carrying a blaze that he had never seen from her before, a wild abandon in stark contrast to her usual reserved demeanor.

She moved closer to him, the lines of duty and decorum blurring as she whispered words that would shake his entire existence, the unexpected desire to be close to him, undoing years of self-restraint. "Make love to me," she said, her voice barely above a murmur, filled with a long-repressed hunger.

Even in his wildest dreams, Donovan never imagined such an encounter. His heart pounded louder than the bouncing balls outside, adrenaline urging him to embrace the moment he'd dreamt of. But somewhere between desire and reality, his conscience whispered warnings. The stakes were too high—too risky for both of them.

He wanted her, more than he'd wanted his own freedom, but he knew too well the cost of a stolen moment. Love, he realized, was sometimes best expressed through sacrifice.

"I can't, Isabella," Donovan uttered with torn sincerity. "Not here. Not like this."

She studied his face, the desperation fading into understanding. The moment passed, unresolved, tense with the gravity of what could not be.

The door opened again, returning them to their roles, and as Donovan stepped out into the open air, his secret well kept, he also realized a trap had been avoided. For the envious eyes hadn't missed the unsanctioned meeting and began to spin the gears of their vindictiveness-looking for a way to ensnare Donovan in their web of jealousy..

Yet Donovan, having chosen honor over desire, remained untouchable. In the end, it was those who sought to ruin him that found themselves exposed, their pettiness laid bare for the administration to see.

Time moved on, and so did Officer Garcia. The facility was left with just the memories of her. For Donovan, the echo of that choice

compelled him to look inward—for he had found strength in restraint and integrity in adversity. And with that quiet power, he continued to face each day, knowing that he had remained true to himself, no matter the cost.

The Unveiling of Saul

In the bustling metropolis of Neotropolis, Saul Goodman was a man renowned for his fiery temper and uncompromising attitude against the followers of The Way—a modern adaptation of early Christian teachings that embraced technology and innovation in their spiritual practices. As a high-ranking cybersecurity official for the dominant religious institution of the land, the Techno-Orthodox Church, Saul was feared and respected in equal measure.

With a fervor matched only by his exceptional skills in digital surveillance and counter-hack operations, Saul scoured the city's neon-lit streets and the boundless expanse of cyberspace to root out and dismantle any gathering of The Way, backed by the full authority of the Church. He saw The Way's mesh of ancient wisdom and contemporary application as a threat to the pure traditionalism he upheld.

One fateful day, Saul was commissioned with a critical task: to lead a crackdown operation aimed at the heart of The Way's underground network, far in the urban sprawl's outer sector.. He was to capture their leaders and bring them to the Church's cyber court, where they would face severe sanctions for their digital heresy.

Saul and his specialized team geared up in their sleek enforcement exosuits, eyes aglow with high-tech visors, ready to launch a synchronized strike. Their armored transport hummed through the city on a suspended magnetic track, lightning-fast and eerily silent—befitting of the impending storm they were about to unleash.

As they approached the sector, where intelligence suggested the dissidents were planning a major virtual rally to share their message globally, Saul's anticipation reached a fever pitch. But at that moment, the unexpected happened: a mysterious blinding light suddenly enveloped their transport, bringing the convoy to a standstill. The source was unknown, and it defied all of Saul's understanding of technology.

Through the glaring luminescence, a figure appeared, with a voice that boomed as if amplified by invisible speakers. "Saul, Saul," it said, "why do you persecute me? It's hard for you to kick against the goads." Saul, disoriented and without any of his tools offering clarity, could only muster a confused response: "Who are you?"

"I am the voice of The Way that you try to silence," the figure replied. "But behold! It is time for your true purpose to be revealed."

In that moment, Saul's world changed. His reality rebooted, and the once fervent enforcer found himself filled with an overwhelming sense of peace and comprehension. He understood that his dedication to the pure, unchanging tradition was blinding him from the evolution and growth that The Way embraced—a harmony between the timeless and the

timely.

When his vision cleared, Saul discovered that he had been rendered temporarily blind by the encounter. Assisted by his bewildered team, he was led into the heart of the city he once policed with iron resolve. For days, Saul was confined in darkness, utterly dependent on those around him.. He fasted and reflected deeply on his experience.

It was in this time of vulnerability that a member of The Way, a woman renowned for her compassion and wisdom named Annette, found Saul. She had heard of his transformation and, despite his history, reached out to him in kindness. Annette touched his eyes, and as if rebooting a system, Saul's vision was restored—not just his sight, but his insight into life's complex digital tapestry. Saul understood that he would no longer dismantle but rather build bridges between worlds, between the ancient and the futuristic.

With this newfound calling, Saul Goodman abandoned his former self and adopted a new identity to reflect his radical change.

He became Paul Newpath—a messenger of The Way, imparting teachings of a living faith that thrived amidst the chips and circuits of a digital era. Paul traversed Neotropolis and beyond, not as an enforcer, but as a uniter, helping others integrate the wisdom of old with the possibilities of the new.

From the highest echelons of the Techno-Orthodox Church to the back-alley data havens where the city's outcasts dwelled, Paul spread his message of transformation and hope. His legacy was the dawn of a dynamic spiritual movement, one that honored the past while boldly stepping into the future. In a world where change was inevitable, and the fusion of man and machine had become reality, Paul's journey from Saul Goodman to Paul Newpath became a legendary tale of revelation, reformation, and a unity forged in the crucible of faith and innovation.

The fallen shield

In the shimmering city of high stakes and fast lives, John "The Shield" Marston was a bodyguard whose name was synonymous with unwavering protection and loyalty. A towering figure with a gaze as sharp as his instincts, he safeguarded the lives of the elite with an unblemished record. Money flowed like a river after a storm: fancy cars, gleaming motorcycles, and the affection of those seduced by his world of extravagance.

Life was good, until it wasn't.

Without warning, the world he knew crumbled. Hidden skeletons were dragged out from the depths of his employer's closet, and the Feds were ravenous for a collar. With each association meticulously linked, John's own life unraveled stitch by stitch..The Feds had come knocking, and where there was smoke, there was fire. In their eyes, John was more accomplice than guardian. Before he could comprehend the gale, he found himself caught in a storm of accusations.

The trial was a blur-the pounding gavel echoing the collapse of his empire. Guilty by proximity, they said. The crestfallen bodyguard was sentenced to time behind cold, iron bars, and John's heart was imprisoned by a greater sentence: the distance from his family.

Inside his cell, silence roared with the intensity of the crowds he once mingled among. Shamed and stripped of his former glory, his days became a carousel of routine and reflection. His wealth vanished. The roar of his motorcycles—a ghostly memory. His cars, once a statement of his success, repossessed as if they had never been his.

Through that time, loneliness was a cruel jailer. John missed his family, aching for a semblance of their presence. Despite the chaos he had unwittingly sown, he dared to dream of reunion.

One day, he called home, praying for a connection to the life he lost. The voice on the other end was his sister's, and it carried the heavy news: the trappings of his old life were all but a memory—everything he cherished, gone. His sister's words were a somber eulogy to his former world

.

But in that graveyard of dreams, there was a single flower blooming defiantly against the despair. Saran, his fiancee, who had been in the background of his most triumphant days, stood resilient in his darkest. There were no more glamorous parties or opulent gifts to give, only the stark truth of adversity and the redemption of unconditional love

.

When the smoke cleared, there she was, on the opposite end of the sterile visitor's room glass, her eyes not dimmed by the shroud of his fate, but rather luminous with unwavering commitment. She spoke not of the materials they'd lost, but of the future they still held. In her voice, he found his sanctuary

.

"You're not alone," Sarah affirmed time and time again, her solace seeping through the glass, the steel, the bleakness. "We'll rebuild, together."

Years passed, and the seasons changed both outside and within the confinements of John's world. He emerged not as the bodyguard who had it all, but as a man humbled and rebuilt from the foundations of trial and resilience. His freedom restored, he stepped back into the expanse of a changed world—no pulsing engines to greet him, no wealth to define him.

Yet, he was richer than he had ever been, for by his side was Sarah, a testament to the timeless adage that the grandest riches are not possessed, but shared in the bonds we hold dear.

Together, they sketched the beginnings of a new chapter—one not of flash and facade, but of depth, growth, and authentic connection. United, they walked ahead into a future uncertain but bright with the promise of redemption and the warmth of enduring love

I can't breathe

Beneath the weight of order's hand, In streets where life and strife expand, A voice arose, pained and deep, Cried a soul, "Mr. Officer, I can't breathe."

His plea, a chorus in the night,

Echoed pains of historic spite, A cry that shook the concrete earth, Denouncing the dearth of his own worth.Enshrouded in the colors of authority, Blind to the pulse of human priority,

The officer, unmoved by the beseech, Steeled his resolve, beyond reach."Please," he gasped,"Release my fate,"A plea for mercy before it's too late.

Yet, cold hands grip; the world grew steep,

As he whispered, "I can't breathe."A nation watched, hearts aghast, What seemed a moment, forever cast, In memories, history books, and speech,

"I can't breathe," the lesson to teach.

The streets erupted in voices loud, Protests in cadence with the crowd.For justice, reform, a communal heave, Chanting in unison,"We can't breathe."Let it not be just a fleeting sound

But a movement where love is found, A change to make right what was wrong, To ensure that every breath is strong.Oh Mr. Officer, a nameless dread, Another soul, humanity's thread,

We cannot stand, we cannot leave, Till all can say, "At last, I breathe."

For Teiara "Boogie" Horton

I remember the day we crossed paths,
Doing security at Canaan Towers,
Long shifts, long talks, sharing laughs—
Time slipped by like quiet hours.
You had a way of breaking walls,
Calling me by my name, no disguise.
The only one I let past it all,
You saw the truth behind my eyes.
Now word has come, the hardest blow,
The Lord has called you home to rest.
No chance for me to tell you so,

How much your friendship was the best.
Boogie, my friend, you left too soon,
Without a wave, without goodbye.
But I'll keep your laughter in my tune,
And your spirit will never die.
Though pain runs deep and cuts like glass,
I'll carry you with every stride.
Memories of you will always last,
My sister, my friend, my guide.
So rest in peace, Teiara dear,
Your soul is free, your journey done.
But in my heart you still stay near—
Forever shining like the sun.

From his reflection

In a world spun wide with fates untold, There stood a man, brave and bold,Named Big Dee, strong and constant as the day, Witnessing from afar his daughter's play.

Afia, her name, a spirit bright,Grew up beneath life's ardent light, Seventeen summers swiftly passed, And in her heart, questions amassed.

Unknown to her, in shadows kept, Her father's gaze, it never slept.From distant realms, with quiet sigh, He watched her laugh, he heard her cry.

He marveled at her every stride,The lows, the highs, the roller-coaster ride, Each triumph, each stumble in her life's dance, From afar he cherished every chance..

Her laughter echoed in his ear, A balm to soothe the passing year, Big Dee a fortress of silent cheer, Keeping his bloodline close and dear.

Then came the day, as fate designed, Two lives, once split, were realigned.

Afia's gaze met Big Dee's own, In her eyes, the years overgrown.

"Daughter mine," he softly said,

"Through life's thickets, I've quietly tread.

Carrying hopes, bearing dreams,

Watching over you through unseen streams."

In her heart, where questions swirled, A space for him, slowly unfurled.

The puzzle of past, in pieces laid,

As father's presence cut through the shade.

Now together, hand in hand,

Rebuilding bridges long unmanned, Big Dee, with heart so full and wide, Grateful to be by Afia's side.

For every chapter missed in fright, They turn the page, they reignite.

A father's love, once paused in time, Now sings aloud in life's grand rhyme.

Baby girl

In memory of Natalie "Baby Girl" Jones, a mother's tale unfurls, Once a beacon of might, an unyielding strength in this world.

A strong Black woman, proud and true,

Her spirit shone, a guiding light, piercing through.

Her name was hallowed, a gentle force, Through tumult and trials, she stayed the course.

Big Dee, her son, behind walls so cold, Made a vow to his mother, brave and bold.

From the depths of despair, his promise clear,

"I'll make bail and be there, please hold on, my dear."

But fate, so cruel, paid no heed to the plea, On January sixteenth, cancer set her spirit free.

The battle was fierce, she fought with grace, Yet even the valiant must sometimes leave the race.

Her legacy, though, would never depart,

Embroidered with love in the chambers of a son's heart.

Big Dee's vow, a whispered promise in the night, Became a mission, his guiding star, his light.

For Natalie "Baby Girl", his champion, his queen, He'd honor her memory, keep her dreams evergreen.

Now the skies tell her story, the stars spell her name, Natalie "Baby Girl" Jones, eternally aflame.

For though the Black warrior mother has gone to rest, Her courage, her love, live on in those she's blessed.

So hear her laughter in the rustle of leaves, Feel her embrace in the cool evening breeze.

Big Dee's resolve, to live up to her name,

Ensures Natalie's spirit burns bright, an undying flame.

Black Lives Matter

In a world where equality should reign, There's a wound we've yet to contain.

A cry rings out, both fierce and loud, Echoing long through the gathered crowd.'Black Lives Matter'—voices rise, Against an unjust, cloudy sky.

For the lives of the taken, we yearn, Their stories urge us to learn.From Ferguson to every street,

Their hearts still beat in the chants we repeat.

For Trayvon, Brenna, George, and so many more, We march, we speak, daring to restore.

The dream that Martin Luther King held dear, That one day, all children, no matter the sphere, Would walk together, free of fear, In a land where justice is truly clear.

In the face of challenge, we stand tall, United, we answer humanity's call.

For every life diminished by hate, We strive to right the records of fate.

Our commitment to change must never tire, Our actions ignited by passion's fire.

Equality not just as a word, but as a norm, In societies transformed, reformed.

We must educate, love, and understand, Support each other, hand in hand;

For the sake of a future brightly lit,

We chant, 'Black Lives Matter,' and we will not quit.

The Box I Can't Stop Filling

I've got me a box,
It's bigger than me,
And what will I cram in?
Just wait—you will see!
A blender, a plunger,
A wig made of blue,
A lawn chair, a lamp post,
A left rubber shoe.
A pizza, a toolbox,

A six-pack of Sprite,
A gnome with sunglasses,
Out dancing all night.
I'll cram in a cactus,
A trumpet, a drum,
A gold disco helmet
That shines on my bum.
In goes a typewriter,
Clunky and loud,
A squeaky balloon
That drew quite a crowd.
A waffle iron,
A bowling pin, too,
A giant pink flamingo
That cackles at you.
Oh, what a wild box,
It wiggles and groans,
Crammed full of odd things,
Like sneakers and cones.
And still I keep going,
No pause and no stop...
'Cause stuffing this box
Is the best kind of pop!

No Longer A Ghetto Son

Once upon a time in the rough streets of Chicago, during the challenging crack era, a boy named Marcus was brought into the world. He was a child of the ghetto, where the echo of sirens laced his lullabies, and whispers of danger danced in the alleys.

Marcus's education unfolded in a battered public school system, where neglected facades matched the disheartened spirits within. The linoleum floors were worn thin with the shuffle of despondent students, and the classrooms buzzed with lost potential.

Marcus's teachers, overwhelmed and desensitized, often dismissed him. "You're just another statistic," they'd say, their words as weighty as lead, pulling him further from his dreams. With each disparaging remark, the little light of hope in Marcuss eyes flickered dimmer. They told him he'd never amount to anything—that the world had neither the space nor the patience for another nobody from the

streets.

Defeated and longing for escape, Marcus began to tread the perilous path laid out by his mother. She too had succumbed to the vices that clawed at the hearts of the broken, looking for solace in the deceptive warmth of drugs. Her journey became his, and the cycle of despair revolved without ceasing.

But life, at times, reveals its grace in the unexpected. One fateful day, Marcus's story took an unforeseen turn. While meandering down the graffiti-scribbled streets, memories of his mother's struggles heavy in his heart, he saw her—Angela, the girl who adorned his dreams with smiles and untold promises. She was his childhood crush, a beacon of innocence amidst chaos. Angela had somehow managed to navigate the tempest of the ghetto and emerged unscathed, her eyes still gleaming with the bright future Marcus once envisioned for himself.

Seeing Angela enkindled a fire within Marcus, a blaze that not even the coldness of his past could extinguish. He saw in her the life he could have had, the one he still yearned for deep down. In her gaze, Marcus found redemption, an unwavering clarity that shattered his world of despair.

She represented the possibility of a life free from the chains of addiction, a testament that one's beginning need not dictate their end.

That day, Marcus made a vow. He decided to break the generational curse that ensnared his family and to pave a new path. It was not an easy quest-withdrawal clawed at him with razor-sharp talons, and the shadows of doubt whispered deceitful enticements. But with Angela's image etched in his heart, and the newfound resolve coursing through his veins,

Marcus fought back with a warrior's spirit.

Day by day, he distanced himself from his old life, seeking help from community centers and finding solace in support groups that welcomed him with open arms. They offered him a sanctuary, tools to rebuild himself, and stories of hope that mirrored his own. Through hard work and relentless determination, Marcus earned his high school diploma against all odds, proving those teachers wrong who had so quickly written him off.

After some time, Marcus gathered the courage to talk to Angela, and she saw in him a kindred spirit—a survivor. Together, they became each other's support. Angela encouraged Marcus to further his education, and he did, attending night classes at a local college while holding down a daytime job.

Years passed, and the boy who was once berated by teachers and trapped in a cycle of despair, emerged as a symbol of hope.

Marcus became a beacon for other youths in his community, sharing his tale of transformation. He pursued a career in social work, determined to be the mentor he never had, lifting others from the abyss he once called home.

In the end, Marcus not only rewrote his own narrative but also became a scribe for countless others, penning epilogues of triumph where society had left only blank, hopeless pages. And there, in the heart of Chicago's streets, he found his purpose—not as a nobody, but as a hero forged from the very same streets that tried to break him.

The Bounty Hunter locked down

In the dust-blanketed town of Red Ridge, the silhouette of a man known as Clayton "Cobra" Reed was a welcome sight for some and the bearer of ill fortune for others. A seasoned bounty hunter, Cobra's reputation for tracking down the most slippery of outlaws spread far across the arid scrublands. Yet beneath the brim of his weathered hat and beyond the icy blue steels of his eyes, Cobra held a secret closer than his twin revolvers—a loving family for whom he would breach heaven and hell.

Cobra's wife, Sarah, and his two boys, Eli and

Jonah, were well provided for from the bounties he fetched, but never at the expense of his honor. He was, above all, a decent man with a steadfast rule; no job would ever blemish his soul. He took pride in hunting only those with blood on their hands or deceit in their hearts.

One sultry afternoon, as the sun beat down on

Cobra's leather-clad back, fate played a cruel hand. A simple misunderstanding in the pursuit of a deranged gunslinger led to an unanticipated skirmish with federal deputies who mistook his intent. Shots rang out, and in the ensuing confusion, Cobra was apprehended, cuffed, and hauled away.

The iron bars of the federal penitentiary clanged shut with a reverberating finality that seemed to echo the entrapment of Cobra's spirit. Yet, his resolve did not waver. Behind those bars, he was determined to remain untarnished, to avoid the kind of violence that marked many men's time inside. He had heard tell of the prison's ruthless hierarchy - an ecosystem built upon aggression and toughness where only the strong survived unscathed.

Sarah, during their brief and closely monitored visits, could see the strain in his once fierce gaze softened with a glimmer of tenderness he reserved just for her. "Just keep your head down," she would urge, knowing the kind of man her husband was—proud but not foolish. "Do this for Eli and Jonah. Do this for me."

As days merged indistinctly into weeks and months, Cobra charted a narrow path of solitude. The raucous catcalls of hardened criminals, the metallic clink of chains, and guards' heavy footsteps became the soundtrack of his existence. Cobra knew any overt sign of weakness could beckon a storm of trouble. The yard became a chessboard of potential conflict, but Cobra moved with purpose, always in control. A nod here, a handshake there, keeping the peace without forging any alliances that could backfire.

Not every prisoner wore their menace externally; some sought to turn even the most neutral of men into pawns for their own survival. The prison was rife with these serpent-tongued deceivers who whispered promises or threats concealed within the same breath. Yet, Cobra's integrity had not wavered when he roamed free, and it would not falter now.

One tension-fraught afternoon, as the sun beat down on the exercise yard's endless concrete, an altercation broke out. Two rival factions clashed with the viciousness of cornered animals—a spectacle that could rend any involved man's future to shreds.. As the yard descended into chaos, a choice lay before Cobra: join the affray and risk everything, or uphold the promise he made to his family.

Flashes of Sarah's pleading eyes and the hopeful faces of Eli and Jonah fortified Cobra's resolve. He stepped back from the roiling mass of violence, even as jeers and provocations attempted to snare him. Cobra was playing a longer game for higher stakes than any prison yard brawl could offer.

His steadfastness was noticed. Unbeknownst to him, an observing warden, weary of the cycle of violence, marked Cobra's conduct. In time, this perception led to an opportunity—a chance to negotiate for an early release based on good conduct and the influential testimony of those he'd helped bring to justice.

Finally, the day came when Cobra walked out of the penitentiary's steel maw, not into the arms of loved ones—such open displays would have to wait for the privacy of home—but into the promise of reclaiming what he was forced to leave behind.

Though the world outside had shifted imperceptibly during his time away, the essence of what made him a man—a father, a husband, a protector—remained unbroken.

As he approached the familiar wooden door of his humble abode, a surge of emotion swelled within him. Behind it awaited Sarah's warm embrace, Eli's adventurous tales, and Jonah's boyish laughter. The bounty hunter who'd hunted criminals to support his family had endured his greatest trial and emerged with his honor intact, ready to rebuild anew.

Where Our Stories Meet

Once upon a time, in a bustling city marked by its vibrant diversity and the chaotic harmony of different cultures blending together, there lived a man named Jamal. Jamal had grown up in a close-knit community that valued tradition, family, and the rich tapestry of their cultural heritage. His life was a colorful mosaic of spicy street food, pulsating hip-hop beats, and the enduring warmth of neighborhood gatherings.

Enter Lily, a woman with porcelain skin and a heart full of good intentions but with a worldview as monochrome as her upbringing in a sheltered suburb. When Jamal and Lily's paths crossed, the attraction was instant. The novelty of their differences drew them together like magnets, their love a bridge across a chasm of contrasting experiences.

But the fabric of their relationship was soon strained by the weight of everyday realities.

Lily struggled to wrap her mind around Jamal's cultural expressions, every facet an enigma she was determined to understand, but often through the lens of her own upbringing. She would watch, perplexed, as Jamal greeted strangers with an innate warmth and familiarity that seemed foreign to her. Each time he would say, "It's just respect, babe," but the concept hung between them like a question mark.

Even the clothes Jamal wore became a subject of debate. He had an affinity for bold colors and chains that glimmered with hints of his heritage, a homage to the style icons he had grown up admiring. But to Lily, this was a sartorial puzzle; she couldn't fathom why he wouldn't embrace the more muted tones of her world.

Their home was filled with the rhythmic flow of hip-hop and R&B, a soundtrack that to Jamal's ears felt like home. To Lily, though, it was cacophony, a constant reminder of a rhythm she couldn't quite dance to, her feet never finding the beat.

The most fraught battleground, however, was the care of their child's hair, a curly crown that brought joy to Jamal and bafflement to Lily. He knew the rituals and products, the protective styles and the tender patience required.

But Lily, with her straight locks, found herself lost, the comb in her hand an unwieldy sword she wielded with the best of intentions but poor knowledge.

The tension between them simmered until it boiled over one hot summer day. When Jamal casually asked Lily to pick up a pair of high-top sneakers for him, she couldn't help but comment, "People don't wear high tops in the summer, you know."

That's all it took for Jamal's frustration to overflow. He let out a laugh, not of humor but of disbelief. It wasn't just about the sneakers; it was the accumulation of all the tiny misunderstandings and debates that had been growing between them. He looked at Lily with eyes that pleaded for recognition, for acknowledgment of his world.

"What's so funny?" Lily asked, her defenses rising in the face of his laughter.

"It's not about the shoes, Lily," Jamal said, his voice tinged with a weariness that tugged at her heart. "It's about you not getting it. About you always questioning the culture that's a part of me, the culture that'll be part of our child's identity."

They stood there, on the precipice of a moment that demanded more than laughter or arguments. It was a moment that called for understanding, for listening, for the willingness to embrace a culture not as a challenge to be debated but as a legacy to be celebrated.

The air was tense but pregnant with the possibility of change. Perhaps, with time, they could learn to dance to the same rhythm or at least appreciate the music of each other's worlds, one step at a time.

Harlem Blues

Once upon a time in the vibrant streets of Harlem, NYC, there lived a singer whose voice could soothe the most troubled of Souls. His name was Jackson, and his powerful melodies echoed through the nightlife, weaving through the maze of streetlights and dreams. With a charisma that matched the stars shining above the city skyline, he was admired by his peers and beloved by his fans. Yet beneath his shining exterior lay a turbulent sea of emotions.

Jackson had fallen, hopelessly and irrevocably, in love with a dancer named Dahlia. She was a combination of beauty and mystery, bewitching all who came to see her dance under the dim glow of the sapphire stage lights. Her world was one of smoke and mirrors, a place where hearts were both won and lost within the span of a single song. And to Jackson, she was the epitome of all that was alluring in this world.

Dahlia, however, did not share the depth of

Jackson's affection. She danced for him, laughed with him, even spent long nights talking to him under the stars, but her heart was a fortress that no man's love could penetrate. She was a free spirit, untethered by the bonds of love that seemed to grip so many others.

Driven by the intoxicating mixture of passion and pain, Jackson's performances began to reflect the storm raging within him. His voice, once smooth and controlled, now poured out raw and ragged with emotion. The audiences were entranced by his fervor, yet oblivious to his suffering. Each night, in a haze of applause and adoration, he found only emptiness—for the one person he longed to impress remained unmoved.

In a desperate bid to show the depth of his love, Jackson decided to commit an act that would forever etch his name in her heart. With a trembling hand, he took to the stage one fateful evening, his gaze locked on Dahlia. As the final notes of his most poignant song faded, he stunned the crowd with a gesture that would become legend. With the craze of a man who had nothing left to lose, he severed his own ear, mirroring the act of a tortured artist from another age.

The crowd gasped in horror, but Jackson's eyes never left Dahlia's. He offered the ear to her as a symbol of his dedication, a gift of his very essence. But the gesture backfired spectacularly. Dahlia recoiled in shock and fear, unable to comprehend the lengths to which his obsession had taken him.

Jackson was rushed to the hospital, his act of love becoming his undoing. Dahlia visited him once, her face streaked with tears not of affection, but of pity and sorrow for the broken man before her. She whispered a soft goodbye, knowing their paths could never entwine again.

In the wake of that night, Jackson's music career faded into a somber silence. The man who once filled Harlem with song became a whisper, a cautionary tale of love turned to madness. Though he healed in body, his spirit remained eternally scarred, a hollow shell of the vibrant singer he once was.

As for Dahlia, she too disappeared from the limelight, vanishing like a ghostly apparition into the annals of the city's history.

Some say she left the dancing life behind, others that she performs still, under a new name, in a city far away from the haunting memory of Jackson's love.

And so the tale concludes, a melancholic melody of a man whose love for a dancer soared too close to the sun, leaving him with nothing but the scars of his passion and a story that would forever resonate in the hearts of those who remember the singer from Harlem.

SHELLS+BIG DEE=ZAVION

Once upon a time in the bustling town of Malvern, Pennsylvania, a man named Big Dee was stepping back into the light of the ordinary world after serving time. He wasn't looking for trouble; he was in search of something far more elusive - love.

In his heart, Big Dee knew he had changed. Yet, the reality of his past wasn't something he could simply erase, nor the mundane job at a fast-food joint that he had landed after his release. Ready to dip his toes into the dating pool, Big Dee turned to the digital sea of Plenty of Fish in hopes of finding a soul whose heart would look beyond the cover of his book.

He carefully crafted his profile, a mix of honesty and charm. With each passing day, Big Dee would scroll through the pages, but it was Shell's page that leapt out amidst the sea of faces. A woman with a smile that seemed to kindle hope, her eyes sparkling with a mix of curiosity and strength. They started to message, tentatively at first, like the first fragile tendrils of a vine reaching out.

When Shellz learned about Big Dee's recent stint in jail and his current job, she didn't flinch. She was intrigued by his straight talk and the sense of determination that seemed to ooze through his less-than-perfect story. Agreeing to meet up with him at his workplace was a leap of faith.

As Shellz pulled up to the fast-food joint in her dependable sedan, out strolled Big Dee. But her eyebrows shot up when she saw him drift over to a flashy car parked nearby, an unexpected contrast to his grease-stained uniform. "Do you really work here?" she asked, half teasing, half serious. Her voice dipped in suspicion like a detective questioning a witness. But it was a harmless dance of trust, and Big Dee just chuckled, assuring her his wheels were simply a fortunate secondhand deal.

A week later, Big Dee invited Shellz to a peaceful park in Malvern. Gone was the uniform, replaced by a man who seemed to transform with every step he took away from the fryers and grills. He laid out a picnic with morsels that spoke of care and attention, foods that would never grace the menu where he flipped burgers. It was a slice of simple romance, under the open sky, that set the stage for their growing connection.

Big Dee, he was a smooth talker, had a way with words that could've charmed the leaves off the trees. He almost swept Shellz right out of her senses, but a sudden downpour had other plans, reminding them that even the best-laid plans could be drenched in unexpected reality.

Despite the soaking, Shellz saw something real in Big Dee. As months passed, their fledgling connection grew into a strong, resilient relationship against the odds. They moved in together, filling their home with laughter, debates about the most mundane of things, and a warmth that neither had expected to find.

Six months later, their love was sealed with the birth of a baby boy. Naming him was a war of loving words until they both heard the name "Xavion." It just fit. They nicknamed him "Zay," and from that moment on, they knew their story - a story of second chances and trust, of a fast-food worker and his unexpected princess - was just beginning.

While Big Dee would always have the shadows of his past lurking at the periphery, with Shellz and Zay by his side, he had found a future brighter than any he could have imagined. This was his next chapter, his true release, a story spun from the truths of redemption, love, and a little bit of digital fate.

A new kind of love

In the vibrant city of laughter and lights, there was a young man named Alex, who was often described as a 'golden boy by those who knew him. With his towering skyscrapers of charm, oceans of wealth, and the charisma that could disarm the sternest of hearts, he lived a life many could only dream of. However, with all the luxury that surrounded him, Alex yearned for something all his riches couldn't buy-genuine connection and love.

One evening, at a cozy comedy club tucked away in a bustling street, Alex's eyes fell upon a female comedian named Sara.

She was an enigma, with a sharp tongue and a wit that sparkled brighter than the stage lights. As she owned the stage with her humor, Alex found himself utterly captivated. After the show, brimming with confidence that often came with privilege, Alex approached her with his best lines and most charming smile.

But Sara was not swayed. Every advance he made was met with a laugh and a playful jibe. "Oh, darling," she would say, laughing off his attempts, "you're far too young. You couldn't possibly handle what I have to offer."

Despite her rebuffs, Alex was not deterred. He knew he had to change his approach. So, instead of continuing with his usual flattery, he asked her to join him for dinner, genuinely wanting to get to know her. To his delight, she accepted.

They spent the evening at an elegant restaurant that overlooked the glistening city. The night was filled with rich conversation, unguarded moments, and unexpected depths. A live band played in the background, their jazz tunes setting the mood while their laughter blended with the soulful music.

Afterward, on a mutual and unspoken agreement, they went back to his hotel room. As the night evolved into an intimate exploration, Alex revealed a side of himself Sara had not anticipated. He was tender, passionate, and sang a duet with her desires in a way that left her breathless. It was then that she understood the layers beneath his veneer of youth.

In an intertwining of fervor and tenderness, they found themselves entwined, giving and receiving with a fervency that melted away any preconceived notions. Sara, with an expertise and dedication as though her very soul was poured into the act, gave him a night etched in the stars.

As dawn cast its first light through the curtains, Sara lay in Alex's arms, exhausted and sated, surrendering to sleep. In that cocoon of warmth and soft whispers of the morning, something profound shifted between them.

He drove her home with the city slowly waking up around them. As they reached her place, they shared a goodbye kiss that carried the promise of a beginning rather than an end.

From that day forth, Sara no longer saw Alex as just a boy; instead, she recognized the depth of his character, his strength, and his ability to surprise her. He was, unarguably, a man with skills—not just in a world bounded by the material but in the realms of emotion, passion, and companionship. And as for Alex, he realized that the connection he sought wasn't found in what he had, but in what he had to give—himself, wholly and uninhibitedly.

A new kind of love

In the vibrant city of laughter and lights, there was a young man named Alex, who was often described as a 'golden boy by those who knew him. With his towering skyscrapers of charm, oceans of wealth, and the charisma that could disarm the sternest of hearts, he lived a life many could only dream of. However, with all the luxury that surrounded him, Alex yearned for something all his riches couldn't buy-genuine connection and love.

One evening, at a cozy comedy club tucked away in a bustling street, Alex's eyes fell upon a female comedian named Sara.

She was an enigma, with a sharp tongue and a wit that sparkled brighter than the stage lights. As she owned the stage with her humor, Alex found himself utterly captivated. After the show, brimming with confidence that often came with privilege, Alex approached her with his best lines and most charming smile.

But Sara was not swayed. Every advance he made was met with a laugh and a playful jibe. "Oh, darling," she would say, laughing off his attempts, "you're far too young. You couldn't possibly handle what I have to offer."

Despite her rebuffs, Alex was not deterred. He knew he had to change his approach. So, instead of continuing with his usual flattery, he asked her to join him for dinner, genuinely wanting to get to know her. To his delight, she accepted.

They spent the evening at an elegant restaurant that overlooked the glistening city. The night was filled with rich conversation, unguarded moments, and unexpected depths. A live band played in the background, their jazz tunes setting the mood while their laughter blended with the soulful music.

Afterward, on a mutual and unspoken agreement, they went back to his hotel room. As the night evolved into an intimate exploration, Alex revealed a side of himself Sara had not anticipated. He was tender, passionate, and sang a duet with her desires in a way that left her breathless. It was then that she understood the layers beneath his veneer of youth.

In an intertwining of fervor and tenderness, they found themselves entwined, giving and receiving with a fervency that melted away any preconceived notions. Sara, with an expertise and dedication as though her very soul was poured into the act, gave him a night etched in the stars.

As dawn cast its first light through the curtains, Sara lay in Alex's arms, exhausted and sated, surrendering to sleep. In that cocoon of warmth and soft whispers of the morning, something profound shifted between them.

He drove her home with the city slowly waking up around them. As they reached her place, they shared a goodbye kiss that carried the promise of a beginning rather than an end.

From that day forth, Sara no longer saw Alex as just a boy; instead, she recognized the depth of his character, his strength, and his ability to surprise her. He was, unarguably, a man with skills—not just in a world bounded by the material but in the realms of emotion, passion, and companionship. And as for Alex, he realized that the connection he sought wasn't found in what he had, but in what he had to give—himself, wholly and uninhibitedly.

The Space Where You Where

In the vibrant, soul-beating heart of Harlem, New York, where the nights shimmered with life and the streets echoed with the latest beats, there lived a man named Holiday. It wasn't his birth name; it was a moniker that stuck from his unparalleled knack for throwing the most unforgettable parties. When dusk fell over the city landscape, Holiday would awaken, his mind buzzing with electric ideas to bring the neighborhood alive with celebration.

Before Holiday became synonymous with the city's nightlife, he was just Terry Jenkins, a smooth-talking young man with a love for music and an undeniable charm that could get him into any room. But it was in those rooms, amid the thrall and pulse of music and merrymaking, that Terry found his true calling and became Holiday.

His reputation grew swiftly, leaving other promoters envious of his skill to reel in crowds like a pied piper. Despite competition, there was mutual respect among most, except for a few who couldn't digest Holiday's rapid success.

One night, at a dimly lit jazz club, Holiday met a man who would change his trajectory once more. Dressed in sharp attire and exuding an air of confidence that matched Holiday's own, was a promoter named Diamond Lou.

Diamond Lou was a legend in his own right, thriving in the business with an empire of VIP events and exclusive parties.

"Holiday, you just light the fuse," he'd say. "Come with me, and I'll show you how to make it all blow up!" And blow up it did Diamond Lou introduced Holiday to the high-end scene of champagne and designer suits, where the parties they threw weren't just celebrations, but spectacles, etching their names in the annals of the city's nightlife.

However, as Holiday's fame soared, so did the attention he got from all facets of Harlem's society, including the most dangerous. It was during one of his luxurious soirees that he met her - the wife of a notorious kingpin known as Big Slick. She was the epitome of beauty and danger entwined, and the moment they locked eyes, there was an electric charge that neither

Holiday knew the streets' unspoken rules, yet an inherent rebellious streak, fueled by the night's intoxication, led him to court danger. They began a secret affair masked by the music's blaring and the city's cacophony, a dangerous dance mere blocks away from Big Slick's watchful eyes.

But secrets in Harlem were like whispers in a storm - unheard for a moment, then violent when caught by the wind. It wasn't long before Holiday's name was mentioned in hushed tones, not for the allure of his parties, but for whispers of betrayal.

A few dudes from his block, loyal to Big Slick, caught wind of the rumors. They couldn't stand the thought of Holiday, once a neighborhood hero, now tangling with Harlem's most feared figure's personal life. So, under the darkness of a new moon, they confronted Holiday.

"Stay away from her, Holiday. You ain't immortal just 'cause you throw parties that make the heavens jealous," they warned, fists clenched and hearts thundering with the threat of violence.

Holiday, whose charm had often been his shield, found his smooth-talking dulled by the gravity of his actions. He realized then the high stakes of his dalliance and the precarious position it put not just himself, but his entire legacy in. He was known for uniting people in celebration, not dividing them with scandal.

The confrontation was a turning point for Holiday. He saw the path he was on could end with more than just a soiled reputation; it could dismantle everything he'd built with the Harlem community. Faced with this grim possibility, Holiday decided to step back from the affair.

He focused on what he knew best - throwing the biggest and best parties that Harlem had ever seen. He channeled his passion into his work, using the near-miss as a hard-learned lesson. Holiday's parties became about more than thrills; they became a testament to the joys of life and the strength of community.

In the end, Holiday managed to restore his respect among his neighbors. The dust settled, and while Big Slick and his own remained ever wary, a mutual understanding kept the peace.

Holiday continued to navigate the world he loved with newfound wisdom and the same old flair, knowing that the true life of the party was not just the celebration, but the unity and harmony it

The Second hand man

Once upon an evening dusk, in the weathered, vibrant streets of Brooklyn, where graffiti murals color the stories of countless souls, a seasoned NYPD con named Detective Mike Russo readied himself for another night on duty. The locker room buzzed with the routine clamour of officers changing shifts, the air thick with purpose and subtle camaraderie.

Mike glanced over the shoulder of his coworker, Detective Marcus Brown, catching a glimpse of a girl's face on Marcus's phone

- she was all smiles and animated gestures, brightening the screen with her charm during a Face Time call.

"Who's that cutie you're chatting with?" Mike asked casually, navigating the delicate line between friendly banter and prying.

"That?" Marcus grinned, locking his gaze with Mike's. "That's my baby mother, Tasha."

Mike raised an eyebrow, a mix of surprise and intrigue painted across his face. He knew better than to encroach on personal relationships within the force, and yet something about the woman's vibrancy captivated him.

Marcus caught the lingering look and, with a mischievous tilt of his head, offered, "You want me to hook you up?" Without much thought, the words "Hell yeah" spilled from Mike's lips.

So Marcus, perhaps driven by his own mysterious motives, shared Tasha's number, and soon enough, Mike was threading words into conversations with her. They exchanged life stories, laughed over shared quirks, and danced around the spark that had been struck between them.

In a whirlwind, Mike and Tasha planned to meet. Under the gleam of streetlights and pulsing city life, they shared dinner at a cozy bistro that echoed with jazz, the melody wrapping around them like a promise. Later, they caught a movie, sitting shoulder to shoulder, sharing chuckles and popcorn as flickering images played before them.

The evening naturally unraveled into a more intimate setting as they found themselves at Mike's place. The night's energy transformed into tender touches and exploration; a dance of desire unfolding effortlessly. His hands etched paths along her skin, drawing soft sighs from Tasha as he found her neck, her sweet spot, prompting her to reciprocate with kisses mapped over his body.

The magnetic pull between them intensified, and with consented urgency, Tasha's hands worked at the fabric of his shirt, tugging it free. His belt clanked softly, a prelude to her unbuttoning his pants.

As garments fell aside, a silent exchange of captivated looks - in Tasha's eyes, a wide-eyed wonder; in Mike's, a raw vulnerability. On a stream of mutual yearning, Tasha maneuvered with grace and ardor, ready to explore and enliven the sensations they were diving into together.

However, the details thereof are sacred, known only to Mike and Tasha, for where passion blooms and intimate moments unfold, privacy veils the scene. What transpired that night remains woven in the silent hours of Brooklyn's embrace, as both individuals connected on a level far deeper than the city's rambunctious facade, finding solace and escape within each other's presence, carving out their own narrative within the city's vast anthology of lives interlacing under the watchful

Unexpectedly

Once upon a time in a small coastal town, there lived a girl named Isabella. With her golden locks that shone like the sunlight and her ocean-blue eyes that mirrored the depths of the sea, Isabella was the epitome of grace and beauty. She was not only pretty in appearance but also kind-hearted, a soul that radiated warmth and innocence.

Isabella's days were filled with simple joys - reading under the shade of the old elm tree, volunteering at the local animal shelter, and laughing with her friends at the town's modest coffee shop. Everyone adored her, and she treaded through life with a gentle certainty, untouched by malice or deceit.

However, Isabella's world was about to be changed by the arrival of a stranger. A young man named Cole rode into town one day, astride a roaring motorcycle that disrupted the stillness. His leather jacket flapped in the wind, and his dark hair was tousled, giving him an aura of defiance and mystery. Cole's reputation roared ahead of his exhaust—he was known to be a loner, a rebel with a past that was spoken of in hushed whispers.

At first, Isabella paid him no mind, her life comfortably ensconced within the protective boundaries of her familiar world. But fate has a funny way of entwining lives, and it wasn't long before Isabella found herself face-to-face with the town's newest enigma.

It was a rainy afternoon when Isabella's car decided to give up, leaving her stranded on the outskirts of the town. As luck would have it,

Cole rode by at just that moment, and despite the rumors, she saw a glimmer of kindness in

his eyes. He stopped, offering her a ride back to safety. Hesitant at first, Isabella accepted, straddling the back of his motorcycle, her arms wrapped reflexively around his waist.

The ride was a revelation. The closeness, the wind against her skin, the exhilarating sense of speed; it was a world away from the confines of her life. As they talked, Isabella discovered a depth to Cole that no one else had seemed to notice. He spoke with a passion about his love for classic literature and his dreams to escape his past and build a new future.

In the ensuing days, the town buzzed with gossip about the pretty girl who had captured the bad boy's attention. Isabella and Cole began to spend more time together, and she saw past his rough exterior to the soul that lay hidden beneath. She learned of the challenges he faced, the struggles that had shaped him, and the gentle heart that beat under his bad boy facade.

Isabella's affection for Cole stirred something within her - a yearning for a life less ordinary, a desire to break free from expectations. With Cole, she laughed louder, dreamed bigger, and dared to peer over the edge of her own limitations.

Yet, love like theirs was not without challenges. Friends and family warned Isabella, cautioning her against falling for someone so seemingly different from her. Cole, too, wrestled with his own demons, the fear that he would only pull Isabella into his troubled world. The two faced criticism and skepticism, their stark contrasts becoming the talk of the town.

But love does not heed the murmur of onlookers. As the seasons changed, the connection between Isabella and Cole only deepened. They balanced each other: where she was softness and light, he brought strength and shade. He showed her the beauty in the wild and unruly, while she taught him the strength found in vulnerability and truth.

In the end, Isabella and Cole proved that love knows no stereotypes; it doesn't conform to narratives or cliches.

True love is the bravery to see the beauty within, to embrace the journey of discovery, and to write a story that belongs solely to those who live it. They didn't know what the future would hold, but under the sprawling elm tree where they had first planned their dreams, they knew they would face it together - the pretty girl and the bad boy, whose love was anything but ordinary.And so, their story continued, a testament to the unexpected and wondrous ways of the heart, unwritten and undefinable, unfolding one sunrise at a time in the small coastal town that had borne witness to their tale.

A HARLEM NIGHT RHYTHM

In the pulsing heart of Harlem, New York, Dangles owned the night. With every we-at of the music and thrust of his hips, he could make the room sizzle, his body a tool of tantalizing temptation. He was the king of the strip scene at Club Euphoria, his stage name echoing through the dark corners of the bustling city.

Dangles wasn't just a performer; he was an artist, painting pictures of desire in the imaginations of those who watched him. A muscular sculpture in motion, his stage presence was as magnetic as his smile; alluring enough to keep an array of eyes glued to him throughout his performances. However, on this particular night, one pair of eyes was notably elsewhere.

She was perched on a stool towards the back, the glow of her phone screen illuminating her face in the dimly lit club. Her focus resided in the digital world trapped within that handheld device. A woman of the 9-to-5 grind, her daily uniform a stark contrast to the glitter and glam of the club - a badge, ID, and peaked cap marked her as an employee of the New York City Transit system.

Dangles could tell that she didn't belong to this world of sin and skin, she was like a dove amidst peacocks. Intrigued and never one to shy away from a challenge, he made his approach. There was a grace to him even when he wasn't on stage. Weaving through the adoring crowd, he arrived at her side and cleared his throat, and with that subtle introduction, her attention was caught, captured, and redirected from her online portal to him.

"Why aren't you enjoying the strip show?" he asked, his voice carrying the confidence of a man used to being the center of attention. She looked up into his eyes, and Dangles was struck by her mixture of innocence and strength..

Smiling, she replied, "No, not at all. Checking in with a husband or anything like that."

Dangles saw the opportunity and took it, a playful glint in his eye. "It's not like you haven't seen everything we have to offer, or is

She laughed, a sound that cut through the bass and rumbled beats. "Perhaps. I guess it's easy to forget that your job is to provide a fantasy," she mused, her thoughts trailing off.

At that moment, Dangles decided to reveal a little bit of his true self. "A fantasy your man can't," he offered, handing her one of his business cards... She took it, and for the first time, Dangles hoped she would use it.

Weeks passed. The business card remained in her wallet, a reminder of the encounter, until one day, when the monotony of her routine cried out for a splash of excitement, she made the call. Their worlds - so different, so apart - collided over dinner in a cozy bistro downtown.

Conversations flowed like fine wine, and laughter came as easy as breathing. Dangles revealed his aspirations beyond the world of titillation - a world where he was known by his given name, Marcus. She shared stories of the Poconos, where she resided now, far from the city that had sculpted them both. They found common ground, their roots both sunk deep into the New York soil of Harlem and Brooklyn, where growing up was as tough as it was transformative.

Date led to date, and it wasn't long before a dance that had started in a club became one of the heart. They twirled into each other's lives with abandon. Dangles, the master of fantasy, found himself caught up in a reality far sweeter than any performance - the reality of love. And she, the lady of transit, found her journey taking an unexpected yet beautiful detour.

In the end, they didn't just find passion; they found a shared rhythm, a unanimous beat in two hearts that had once echoed alone. Dangles no longer just owned the night; he shared it, under the stars of the Poconos, with the woman who rode in on a transit card and left with his heart.

The City of Brotherly Love

In the heart of the eastern seaboard of the United States, there lies a city steeped in history and cloaked under the mantle of camaraderie - the city they call Brotherly Love. Nestled along the banks of the Delaware River, Philadelphia, was a tapestry where the threads of time and unity formed a pattern of profound significance.

It was on a brisk autumn morning when young Elijah set out to explore the cobblestoned streets that George Washington once traversed. The city's soul whispered to him in the crisp breeze that danced through the fluttering leaves of the sycamore trees lining the historic pathways. He was a newcomer, having moved under the allure of Philadelphia's rich cultural tapestry and its infamous reputation for welcoming hearts and open arms.

As he meandered through the bustling markets of South Street, his senses were greeted with the harmonious cacophony of hawkers peddling their vibrant wares, the delectable aroma of cheesesteaks sizzling on the griddles, and the melodic tunes of street musicians that resonated with a touch of jazz and a dash of soul. He witnessed smiles being exchanged, not as currency, but as a silent vow that spoke of unity and kinship among the city's denizens.

His journey escorted him to the legendary Liberty Bell, its infamous crack a testament not to imperfection but to the endurance of freedom that rang through the ages. It was here that Elijah met Anna, a volunteer historian, who spoke with a passion that gave voice to the struggles and triumphs woven into the very fabric of the city. With every tale, she illustrated the depth of connection that

Philadelphians shared, reaching back to the uncertain days of revolution, through times of war and peace, of division and reconciliation.

As the sun embarked on its westward descent, casting orange hues upon the city's skyline, Elijah found himself at the steps of the Philadelphia Museum of Art. Still brimming with energy and a curious spirit, he ascended the steps with a steady pace - each stride feeling like a crescendo building up within him. Atop, he turned to gaze upon the expansive view before him; it was a panoramic spectacle of the picturesque city that had taken him under its wing.

Down below, the verdant swath of Fairmount Park brought together families, friends, and strangers. The young and the old played, laughed, and shared stories in a multitude of languages, yet each conversation was underpinned by the city's universal language - brotherly love.

As twilight approached, Elijah found his way to Independence Hall. It stood like an aging sage, its red brick walls a silent chronicle of the city's pledge for liberty and justice for all. He realized that brotherly love did not solely reside in the physical embrace or the shared laughter among the city's inhabitants; it was etched in the very principles upon which Philadelphia was founded.

As the stars began to unveil themselves in the night sky, Elijah understood that the city's true

love story was not just his alone but an ongoing narrative shared by millions who had walked these streets.. It was love encapsulated in mutual respect, in fighting for what is right, in the helping hand extended beyond prejudice and circumstance, in the vow to lift and uphold one another.

Indeed, Philadelphia was not simply called the City of Brotherly Love because of its founders' Quaker origins or the translation of its Greek name. It was the living embodiment of the idea, resonating through time, brick, and soul. Every monument, every street, every face told a story of love, brotherhood, and the unwavering spirit of humanity. And as Elijah finally retreated to his new home in this kindred metropolis, he carried with him the warmth of brotherly love that would forever beat in the heart of Philadelphia.

Hope Revised

Once upon a time in a bustling city overshadowed by towering skyscrapers and endless commotion, there lived a troubled preteen named Sophia. Sophia's life was anything but easy; her days at school were marked by ridicule and harsh mockery from her peers. Laughter at her expense echoed through the corridors, piercing her like thorns. As the bullying intensified, Sophia's innocence began to fade, and the bright light of her youth dimmed.

Feeling isolated and desperate for a sense of belonging, Sophia found herself unwittingly slipping into the city's shadowy underbelly - a world where the rules of right and wrong blurred like the graffiti on the alley walls. She befriended a group of older kids who, cloaked in the allure of rebellion, introduced her to petty crime. Sophia convinced herself that the adrenaline rush was a remedy for her pain, that the clink of stolen money was the sound of

acceptance.

But deep inside the chambers of her heart, a

battle raged. Whispers of doubt rose above the clamor of her new lifestyle. She'd lie awake at night, the weight of her actions pressing on her chest, making it hard to breathe. A silent cry for redemption echoed in her mind. One fateful evening, enveloped in the solitude of her room, Sophia crumbled to her knees, her tears soaking the carpet beneath her.

"God," she pleaded, feeling the cracks in her facade widen, "I know I've lost my way. I'm scared, and I don't know how to turn back. Please, help me."

In the stillness of her surrender, something within her stirred. A wave of warmth rushed over her—an indescribable peace that wrapped around her like a gentle embrace.

She knew in that moment that she was not alone, and a sense of forgiveness began to heal the wounds of her soul. She felt born again, as if she had been given a new start.

Sophia's transformation was profound. She sought a new refuge, a church home that welcomed her with open arms and hearts filled with compassion.

The community there fostered her growth, and

they became the family she never knew she needed. In this sanctuary, as she healed, Sophia found purpose. She began to share her testimony, her voice a beacon of hope for those veiled in despair.

Her story resonated with many, and soon, she became a pillar of strength within the congregation. She recognized a chance to give back, to guide others away from the precipice she once stood upon. Sophia signed up as a mentor, eager to extend a lifeline to pre-teens caught in the same storm of bullying and misguided choices that once raged through her life.

With patience and love, Sophia reached out to them, offering her lessons as a map to safer shores. She did not sugarcoat her past; instead, she painted it with honest strokes, illustrating the power of second chances and the grace that saved her.

Through her enduring faith and unwavering dedication, she watched as, one by one, the teens she mentored began to turn towards the light of better paths..

Sophia's life, once riddled with strife, had transformed into a remarkable journey of redemption and service. In the heart of the city that had tested her, she became a beacon of hope, a testament to the power of forgiveness and the never-ending grace that had guided her home.

Another kind of concrete

Once upon a time in Brooklyn, New York, there was a man named Gabriel Torrent. He was an enigma, with a quiet disposition and an unassuming appearance, yet inside him brewed a storm of dark impulses. Gabriel grew up in the digital era, a time when the world was interconnected through screens and social media platforms. But rather than use these tools to build bridges, Gabriel constructed a labyrinth of terror.

As a child, Gabriel was often overlooked and neglected, his voice drowned out by the constant buzz of the city. He found solace in the anonymity of chat rooms and forums, where he could don a mask and be anyone he desired. But as time went on, the mask began to fuse with his skin, the lines between reality and the digital persona blurring.

When Gabriel reached adulthood, he was a man divided. By day he wandered the ever-busy Brooklyn streets, a ghost among the living. But by night, he soared across the digital landscape, his presence felt globally. Despite the countless interactions, Gabriel never formed true connections. That is until fleeting messages started to invade his solitude - curious internet denizens seeking connection, not knowing they were flirting with danger.

They called him "The `Nomad," a name he embraced. To the world, it represented his love for travel, as he shared breathtaking images from cities around the globe. However, beneath the curated gallery of beautiful landscapes and exotic landmarks, there lurked a sinister agenda. The Nomad was on a hunt, not for sights, but for victims.

The pattern was always the same. He'd receive a direct message, a stray comment, or some form of digital outreach. But rather than reply with kindness or dismiss the interaction, Gabriel would meticulously research the person behind the screen. Utilizing his skills in hacking and social engineering, he unearthed addresses, routines, and, critically, when they would be most

His travels were a morbid tour with a dark purpose. He'd arrive in a new city, not to see the sights, but to stalk his prey—those unfortunate souls who had dared reach out to him casually, naively. He'd study them, follow them, and when the moment was just right, they would disappear, leaving behind a digital ghost where once there was a thriving presence

The media dubbed him "The Social Media Killer." They reported on the shocking vanishings, the stark silences where once vibrant online personas had been. Fear swept across platforms as users began to question the potential horrors that might be lurking behind every friend request and direct message.

Yet, amidst the chaos, Gabriel felt an insatiable hunger growing. The thrill of the hunt was addictive, but it was also spiraling out of his control. He was no longer the puppeteer; he had become the puppet to his dark desires.

As his list of victims grew, so did the efforts to catch him. Digital forensics teams, international law enforcement agencies, and cybersecurity experts all worked in a frantic race against time to track down the elusive killer before he could strike again.

In the end, it was the very platform he had used to select his victims that became his downfall. A meticulous pattern emerged from the data, a digital signature that he had inadvertently left behind. And when authorities finally caught up with Gabriel in a small cafe in Prague, the faces of his pursuers were not unlike the avatars of those he had once stalked: surreal, yet all too real

.

Gabriel Torrent was brought to justice, his reign of terror brought to an abrupt halt. The world grew a little wiser, a little more cautious in the wake of his capture. Social media users began to embrace anonymity with respect, understanding the vulnerability that came with visibility.

The story of Gabriel Torrent, the man from Brooklyn who became a global predator, serves as a chilling reminder that behind the veil of digital interaction, reality remains, as does the potential for darkness. It's a tale that echoes through the tweets, posts, and updates, whispering to us to tread carefully in the vast, connected world we have built.

The Blueprint of a Man

In a bustling modern-day city, there lived a father who had built a flourishing business from the ground up. He had two sons, Alex and Bryan, who were as different in their ways as night and day. Alex was a free spirit, always seeking adventure, while Bryan was meticulous and devoted to his studies.

One crisp autumn morning, the father called his sons into his sleek, glass-walled office that overlooked the skyline. As they settled into plush leather chairs, the father said,

"My sons, I need your help. Our family business is launching a community development project, an initiative to create a park that would bring green space to the heart of our concrete jungle."

Turning to Bryan first, he asked, "Will you manage this project for me?" Bryan, with his laptop already open to a strategy game, replied promptly, "Of course, Father. I'd be happy to take care of it." Pleased, the father gave Bryan all the necessary details and documentation to

start the work.

Next, the father turned to Alex, who was peering distractedly through the window at the buzzing streets below. "And Alex, will you help your brother in this task?" But Alex shook his head.

"Sorry, Dad. You know that's not my thing. I've got plans with my

friends and adventures to find." The father nodded quietly, a tinge of sadness in his eyes,

but he respected his son's honesty.

As the day waned, Bryan remained in his father's office, absorbed in his digital battles and strategies, ignoring the project he had promised to undertake. It was in the quiet of his room that evening, amidst a pile of travel gear and photography equipment, that Alex had a change of heart.

The image of his father's disappointed face tugged at his conscience. With a sigh, he picked up the phone and dialed the family business's foreman. "Hey, it's Alex. I'll be taking over the park project. Let's meet first thing in the

morning."

True to his word, Alex rose with the dawn and threw himself into the work. Under his fresh and enthusiastic leadership, the park began to take shape: trees were planted, walkways paved, and benches installed. The community watched as what was once a grey patch of earth transformed into a vibrant oasis in the city.

Meanwhile, Bryan stayed comfortably in his routine, contributing nothing to the project he had promised to lead. He often glanced at his father's disappointed expression, yet couldn't bring himself to act.

When the ribbon-cutting day arrived, the father stood before the beautiful new park, the community buzzing around him, grateful for the new space. Alex and Bryan were both at his side. The father addressed the gathering, "This park stands as a testament to the good we can do when we act on our promises and work together. It is not our words but our actions that shape the

After the applause faded, the father turned to his sons. To Bryan, he said softly, "I wish you had followed through on your word." And to Alex, with a proud and grateful smile, he added, "And you, my son, have shown me that it is never too late to do the right thing. You have made your old man very proud today."

The lesson had come full circle for both brothers, and the truth of their father's words would echo in their hearts.

They learned that while one may speak with conviction, it is the quiet turn of the heart and the ensuing actions that truly define commitment and character. And in the heart of the city, the green park stood as a sanctuary, a reminder that in the midst of life's ceaseless hustle, there can still be a place of serenity and beauty born of genuine intent and labor.

The Instant Connection

Once upon a time, in a bustling city marked by its vibrant diversity and the chaotic harmony of different cultures blending together, there lived a man named Jamal. Jamal had grown up in a close-knit community that valued tradition, family, and the rich tapestry of their cultural heritage. His life was a colorful mosaic of spicy street food, pulsating hip-hop beats, and the enduring warmth of neighborhood gatherings.

Enter Lily, a woman with porcelain skin and a heart full of good intentions but with a worldview as monochrome as her upbringing in a sheltered suburb. When Jamal and Lily's paths crossed, the attraction was instant. The novelty of their differences drew them together like magnets, their love a bridge across a chasm of contrasting experiences.

But the fabric of their relationship was soon strained by the weight of everyday realities. Lily struggled to wrap her mind around Jamal's cultural expressions, every facet an enigma she was determined to understand, but often through the lens of her own upbringing. She would watch, perplexed, as Jamal greeted strangers with an innate warmth and familiarity that seemed foreign to her. Each time he would say, "It's just respect, babe," but the concept hung between them like a question mark.

Even the clothes Jamal wore became a subject of debate. He had an affinity for bold colors and chains that glimmered with hints of his heritage, a homage to the style icons he had grown up admiring. But to Lily, this was a sartorial puzzle; she couldn't fathom why he wouldn't embrace the more muted tones of her

world.

Their home was filled with the rhythmic flow of hip-hop and R&B, a soundtrack that to Jamal's ears felt like home. To Lily, though, it was cacophony, a constant reminder of a rhythm she couldn't quite dance to, her feet never

finding the beat.

The most fraught battleground, however, was the care of their child's hair, a curly crown that brought joy to Jamal and bafflement to Lily. He knew the rituals and products, the protective styles and the tender patience required. But Lily, with her straight locks, found herself lost, the comb in her hand an unwieldy sword she wielded with the best of intentions but poor knowledge.

The tension between them simmered until it boiled over one hot summer day. When Jamal casually asked Lily to pick up a pair of high-top sneakers for him, she couldn't help but comment, "People don't wear high tops in the

summer, you know."

That's all it took for Jamal's frustration to overflow. He let out a laugh, not of humor but of disbelief. It wasn't just about the sneakers; it was the accumulation of all the tiny misunderstandings and debates that had been growing between them. He looked at Lily with eyes that pleaded for recognition, for acknowledgment of his world.

"What's so funny?" Lily asked, her defenses rising in the face of his laughter.

"It's not about the shoes, Lily," Jamal said, his voice tinged with a weariness that tugged at her heart. "It's about you not getting it. About you always questioning the culture that's a part of me, the culture that'll be part of our child's identity."

They stood there, on the precipice of a moment that demanded more than laughter or arguments. It was a moment that called for understanding, for listening, for the willingness to embrace a culture not as a challenge to be debated but as a legacy to be celebrated.

The air was tense but pregnant with the possibility of change. Perhaps, with time, they could learn to dance to the same rhythm or at least appreciate the music of each other's worlds, one step at a time.

Where Our Color's Meet

Once in a small, picturesque town nestled in the gentle curve of a river, there lived a white woman named Sarah. She was the younger of two daughters in the Matthews family, a family held in high esteem by the town for their philanthropy and community service. Yet, beneath the surface civility of their refined southern demeanor, the Matthews held views that were very much at odds with the progressive world evolving around them

.

Sarah's parents, Thomas and Elizabeth, had instilled in their children the conservative values they had themselves been brought up with, which included certain prejudices. Their older daughter, Emily, had absorbed these biases and was quite vocal about them. On the other hand, Sarah had always felt a quiet rebellion stir within her, fueled by a sense of justice and empathy that she couldn't quite trace the origin of.

As Sarah grew into a young woman, she found herself drawn to the warmth and vibrancy she observed in the culture of her black peers. Although she had been raised in an environment that did not engage deeply with black culture, there was an allure, an authenticity, she found herself inescapably attracted to.. It was at the town's annual Autumn festival that she met James.

James was volunteering at one of the booths, his infectious laugh reaching Sarah long before she saw his face. When they finally did meet, her pale cheeks flushed a rosy pink as his deep brown eyes met hers. They soon struck up a conversation and Sarah found herself entranced by his passion for music, art, and a world she found both beautiful and quite unfamiliar.

Over time, their friendship blossomed into romance, although Sarah kept it a secret from her family, sensing their disapproval.

When she finally mustered the courage to introduce James to her family, the air was tense. Her parents cloaked their distaste in polite smiles, yet she could feel the chill of their judgment. Emily took little effort to disguise her disapproval and discomfort.

Despite her family's silent, and sometimes not-so-silent objections, Sarah continued her relationship with James. It wasn't just about defiance. James was warm, understanding, and patient, even when Sarah made missteps in her understanding of his culture. He opened her world to the rich history and heritage of his ancestry, teaching her about the struggles and triumphs of the black community. Sarah's eyes were opened to a reality she'd been shielded from, and she grew in empathy and awareness.

Eventually, Sarah and James decided to start a family. The birth of their children brought both joy and complexity to the family Jvnamics. Sarah's parents were faced with a choice: cling to their prejudices or embrace their grandchildren. While they struggled with their own ingrained biases, the innocence of their grandchildren began to thaw their hearts.

Emily found it hardest to conceal her disdain. Yet as the kids grew, they would ask their aunt questions, reach for her hand, or laugh in ways that reminded her so much of Sarah that she, too, could not remain entirely untouched. She was forced to confront the "fuckery"—as Sarah sometimes referred to the complex, messy challenge of navigating family prejudices—that her own stance had added to family gatherings.

Through a series of small, everyday incidents and conversations—shared meals, birthdays, graduations—prejudices began to erode. Sarah's family slowly came to understand that love was more important than their preconceived notions of acceptable relationships and appearances. The love Sarah and James showed each other, and the joy their children emanated, acted as a mirror reflecting the unnecessary bitterness and division that their biases upheld.

In time, Sarah's family learned to accept, and even celebrate, the differences they had once feared. The children grew up at the intersection of diverse cultures, enriched by their mixed heritage. Sarah and James's love story, built on patience and understanding, became a testament to the power of love to overcome ignorance and prejudice.

It was a complex journey, fraught with tension and the need for growth but woven throughout with the unyielding threads of love.. The family was not perfect, their prejudices not entirely vanished, but they were learning, evolving, and most importantly, opening their hearts. And it was in this opening, this willingness to change, that hope found its place at the Matthews family table.

Second Chance

Once upon a time in the vibrant, bustling streets of North Philadelphia, there was a woman named Ava. She was a woman who, despite the few relationships she had been in, was scarred by a history of infidelity. Each time she wandered into the arms of another, it was an attempt to fill a void that seemed endless. When the truth inevitably surfaced, the relationships crumbled like aged brickwork, leaving her with feelings of guilt and emptiness.

Ava's experiences led her to erect walls around her heart, thick and fortified like the steel doors of the towering warehouses scattered across Philly's industrial landscape. They were barriers born from a fear of burdening another soul with her mistakes and an even greater fear of once again shattering her own fragile heart. So, she resolved to keep her distance, diving into work and family, avoiding the complexities of romantic love.

Enter Damien, a man who was no stranger to having his life under control. He ran a barbershop in North Philly, a spot that buzzed with the daily hum of clippers and the warm chatter of a loyal clientele. It was through one of these clients, Ava's cousin, that Damien's path crossed with Ava's.

Their first meeting was happenstance - a family barbecue where the smoky tang of grilling meats filled the air and laughter echoed between homes tightly packed along narrow streets. Damien saw her across the yard, her smile as warm as the September sun. She greeted him with a polite nod, her guard visibly up, her eyes an unreadable mask.

Intrigued and undeterred, Damien set out to know Ava better. As fate would have it, their paths kept crossing - at neighborhood events, through mutual acquaintances, and random encounters at the local market. He met her family members, who quickly took a liking to him, yet this connection brought him no closer to penetrating Ava's defenses.

Despite the barricade surrounding her heart, Ava could not ignore the quiet strength Damien exuded. He seemed genuine, constantly sharing stories of his life and asking nothing of her but friendship. He made her laugh, a rich, genuine sound she hadn't heard from herself in years. Yet the walls remained.

Damien began to sense the warmth behind Ava's cool facade and realized that her reluctance wasn't indifference, but fear. He approached her one crisp evening outside her grandmother's house, the streetlights casting a golden glow on the sidewalk.

"Ava," he said calmly, his eyes holding hers, "I know we've danced around it, but I have to tell you. I have feelings for you. Real feelings." The words left him with a vulnerability he didn't often show.

Ava looked at Damien, her heart thumping against her ribcage. "I don't know if I can do this..." she whispered. "I have a past that's messy. I'm trying not to hurt anybody anymore, including myself."

Damien stepped closer, his presence a comforting warmth. "I'm not asking for you to break down your walls in a day," he replied.. "But maybe, just maybe, we could start by building a doorway—a small one, one that you can open and close as you please. I'll be here, whenever you're ready to let me in, even if it's just a crack."

Ava looked at him, the earnestness in his eyes echoing the sincerity in his words. For the first time in a long time, she felt a flicker of hope, the possibility of something real and uncomplicated. And while she was afraid of the unknown, she was also tired of the loneliness that came with being fortified behind her self-made barricades.

Over time, the crack grew, moments shared led to trust, and trust led to a grudging admission of her own growing feelings.

Damien never rushed her, never wavered in his gentle pursuit. North Philly watched as autumn leaves turned to snowflakes, and slowly, very slowly, Ava began to dismantle the wall, brick by brick, letting Damian's love fill the spaces in between. It wasn't easy, but perhaps, in this story of second chances, it wasn't the ending but the journey of healing and vulnerability that mattered most.

A Familiar Ghost

Once there was a married woman named Isabella, whose heart was caught in tumultuous crosswinds of the past and present.

Her marriage with Michael had once been a tale of storybook romance, but as the years slipped into a comfortable monotony, Isabella's thoughts often drifted to the what-ifs of bygone relationships—the allure of lost love colored with the hue of nostalgia.

In a twist of fate, or perhaps a cruel trick of the universe, Isabella's past resurfaced when she unexpectedly crossed paths with her two former flames, Andrew and David. The encounter was as a spark to dry tinder; old flames were rekindled, and she found herself hopelessly in love with both men once again. Her heart was an aching battlefield, her affections torn between the foundation she had built with Michael and the passion of lost yesterdays.

Conflicted and seeking solace, she contemplated whether to remain tethered to the family she had created or to chase the reminiscence of her former lovers. The wrestle with her conscience was unbearable, and in a moment of desperation, she disclosed her emotional turmoil to Michael.

Her confession was a maelstrom that upended the stability of their marriage. Michael, who had always been a bulwark of strength and patience, now found himself awash with insecurity and anger. His responses to her confessions were laced with acrimony, and the home they had shared became a battleground for tension-charged confrontations.

The cacophony of their discord rang in Isabella's soul, each fight leaving deep scars that yearned for healing. Out of desperation, she sought solace in conversations with Andrew and David. Their familiar voices were balm on her wounds, soothing the hurt caused by her present strife.. With each call, Isabella felt a fleeting respite, but it also deepened her

internal conflict.

Time, however, was an uncompromising force, whispering truths into Isabella's ear as the days flourished and wilted. It dawned on her, amidst the tryst with possibility and the reality of her vows, that she could not walk two paths at once. She knew she must make a choice, and the gravity of the decision lay heavily upon her. This was not merely a verdict of the heart but a defining moment for her integrity and the legacy she wished to leave.

In an epiphany born of deep introspection, Isabella realized that her heart had already made its choice. She wanted a love not just forged in the rosy gleam of the past or the fleeting ecstasy of a clandestine call, but a love tested by the storms of life, strengthened by mutual respect and genuine commitment.

With newfound resolve, she chose her marriage, choosing to rebuild the trust that had been compromised with Michael. It would be a taxing journey, one paved with difficult conversations, counseling sessions, and heartfelt apologies. Isabella understood that Michael's love was worth fighting for and that forgiveness from both sides was necessary for

healing.

She bid farewell to Andrew and David, thanking them for the memories and the brief solace they had provided, but admitting that their chapter in her life was meant to be closed. She pledged to mend the bonds with Michael and focus on the future they had promised each other.

And though the road to reconciliation was long and fraught with challenges, Isabella and Michael slowly and painstakingly revived the embers of their marriage. They learned to communicate with greater honesty, to cherish each other amidst life's cacophony and to foster a love that was not blind to imperfections but was willing to grow beyond them.

In the end, Isabella found that the truest form of healing was not in escaping to the past but in embracing the present with a willing heart and an abiding love.

HER OWN NIGHTMARE

Maria was a maelstrom of fury, as volatile as the ocean during a tempest. Her life was a series of escalating storms, punctuated by violent outbursts that battered everyone in her wake.

As a wife, she had ruled her household through intimidation and fear, her anger an unchained beast that none could tame. Unfortunately, her aggressive nature spiraled out of control, and one fateful night, it led her to commit a crime so heinous it landed her on death row.

In the shadowy confines of the prison, Maria continued to bristle against her chains, her rage unabated even as the consequences of her actions began to loom large. Isolated and irredeemable, she sought solace in a newfound faith, searching for a peace she had never known.

She began to write, the words flowing from her like a stream of consciousness, a purging of the soul that manifested in the form of books.

Despite her inner transformation, her reputation as a volatile soul preceded her.

Officers at the facility, particularly one stubborn and vindictive guard, saw her attempts to change as nothing more than ruses. They subjected her to frequent cell tosses, confiscating her manuscripts and leaving her to rebuild her works from scattered memories and the depths of her tumultuous heart.

Her temper, though somewhat quelled by faith, still flared fiercely. During a routine escort to the recreation yard, she unleashed her fury upon the officer, her venomous words lashing out like whips.

The consequence was immediate; she was banished to the solitary confinement of the Special Housing Unit (S.H.U.), a tomb of silence and reflection.

There, in that isolated cell, it seemed her spirit might finally break. That was until an ethereal presence materialized before her—a being of light, an angel, who whispered to her that it would be alright, that she simply needed to keep the faith.

The encounter left an indelible mark on Maria's soul, imbuing her with a tranquility she had never known.

Four agonizing months later, she was returned to death row. Freshly invigorated by the angelic encounter,

Maria resumed her writing with renewed vigor and passion. However, the same spiteful officer, determined to thwart her aspirations, once again disrupted her cell, scattering her pages to the wind.

That day, fortune's wheel turned. The captain, alerted by the cacophony of conflict, stumbled upon the chaos. Witnessing his subordinate's vendetta, he intervened, admonishing the officer for his unprofessional behavior. The officer, seething with fury, spat venomous threats at Maria, vowing that this was not the end.The captain's stern voice cut through the tension,"I think it

The confrontation escalated in the captain's office, where words gave way to fists as pride and resentment erupted into violence. An officer passing by had to sound his body alarm, resulting in a team of C.E.R.T. officers rushing to quell the brawl.

Luckily, the captain's office was fitted with a camera that captured everything—even the officer making the first aggressive move.

Maria, now truly alone in her struggle to find redemption, could only look on as her world raged around her. It was in this crucible of chaos that she discovered her strength, her faith in the angel's words, and the unyielding resolve to rewrite her story, one word at a time.

The Measure of a Mistake"

In a modern-day city pulsing with the beat of humanity's hurried tempo, there was a woman named Maria who found herself amidst a tempest of disgrace. She worked at a local diner down the dreary alley of Main Street, her life echoing the same monotonous rhythm as the clinking dishes and the swirl of coffee in endless cups.

Maria had made mistakes, ones that the tight-knit community around her found unforgivable. A lapse in judgment had led to an affair, and the news spread like wildfire, igniting disdain in every whisper and glare directed her way. The judgment was fierce and without mercy, and it seemed as if the town had determined her fate, which felt as harsh and irreversible as stones poised to bruise skin and break bones.

One day, as she walked home, her path congested with a crowd holding placards with scathing words, Maria's eyes met with those of a street artist named Joshua. Unlike the others, his gaze held no contempt, but rather an ineffable sadness for the scene before him. He watched as the mob's shouts grew louder, their words as sharp as jagged rocks.

"Shame on you, Maria!" they cried. "You deserve to be punished!"

Just as the air grew tight with the impending doom of Maria's public shaming, Joshua stepped forward and knelt on the sidewalk. With nothing but his finger and the dust motes dancing in the slanted sunbeams, he began to write. The crowd's curiosity swelled, their anger momentarily giving way to the intrigue as Joshua's finger traced characters in the auburn-hued

They leaned closer, trying to decipher what righteous judgment this stranger would etch. Yet it was not an accusation or a decree that the dust held. Instead, Joshua wrote a simple, but profound sentence that hushed the aggrieved throng.

"Let the one among you who has never erred cast the first word of condemnation."

The effect was as immediate as it was uncanny. The crowd fell silent, each individual trapped in their reflection of personal failings and moments they themselves had erred. Shamed by the mirror held up to their own lives, their grip on the condemning placards weakened. One by one, the signs dropped to the ground, creating a patchwork of discarded judgment.

Joshua stood up, and his voice, firm yet compassionate, broke the stillness. "Who among you can claim to be without fault?

Who has never sought forgiveness or a second chance?"

The crowd parted as he continued, "In every heart, there is the capacity for both wrong and for redemption. Today, choose to be the force of understanding and a new beginning for another."

As if chained minds were unshackled, the hostility evaporated, leaving behind a heavy cloud of introspection. The individuals

Maria, tears mingling with a faint smile, walked through the dispersing crowd, feeling lighter than she had in months. Joshua walked beside her, a silent guardian whose presence spoke volumes of the compassion inherent in

humankind.

In the days that followed, the atmosphere of the town began to shift. Whispers of understanding replaced the previous harsh judgments, and many found themselves seeking to mend bridges rather than burn them. Though not all hearts were changed, enough were, and in that change, a ripple of

grace enveloped the community.

Joshua, the artist with a contemplative soul and love for intrinsically flawed humanity, continued to write messages in the dust—not to condemn, but to remind, to heal, and to unite. And Maria found herself, for the first time in what felt like an eternity, living without the

looming shadow of her past mistakes.

For in this modern retelling of an ancient story, the message remained unchanged: The capacity for forgiveness and the human connection stands as the most enduring testament to the better angels of our nature, penned in the sands of compassion and read in the actions of grace.

Faith of the Bronx

Once upon a time in the tough concrete jungle of the Bronx, New York, there lived a little girl named Aliyah Faith Diaz. Aliyah wasn't like other girls her age; she had to navigate the world slightly differently, for she was blessed with a beautiful mind Shaped by autism. With her large, expressive eyes and quick smile, she carried an innocence that starkly contrasted the gritty reality around her.

Aliyah was the middle child of a family bursting at the seams - brothers who were fiercely protective, sisters who were her confidants, and parents who were her rock. Her world was a cacophony of love, laughter, and the daily struggles of life in the Bronx.

As the years ticked by, Aliyah blossomed into a perceptive 15-year-old whose love for numbers made her stand out in school; math class was her sanctuary. The allure of equations and the certainty of mathematical truths gave her a peace not often found in her bustling surroundings.

Then, a tidal wave of misfortune swept over the Diaz household. An unfortunate event snatched Aliyah from the only home she'd ever known, and she was thrust into the cold and indifferent world of a foster home. Here, isolation encircled her as some of her peers, recognizing her difference as weakness, took to bullying. They'd snatch her belongings, taunt her in the halls, and attempt to eclipse her bright spirit.

Back in the Bronx, her father, imprisoned for a minor offense, felt each blow as though it struck his own body. He was known as DJ to his friends and family, and despite his circumstances, he was determined to fight for his daughter. He listened to every story through the prison phone, his heart sinking, and his resolve hardening with each tale of his daughter's suffering. DJ, while dealing with his own barriers, became an invisible pillar of strength for Aliyah, reinforcing her resilience through his encouraging

Aliyah's mother, once overwhelmed by the challenges of raising a large family virtually alone, had now become a ferocious lioness in her efforts to reunite with her daughter. The courts were unyielding, but she knew she couldn't give up.

Finally, on a chilly morning of March 7th, 2024, matters took a turn. The courtroom, with its high ceilings and air of authority, held their collective breath as the Diaz family's fate hung in the balance. Du had managed to secure a compassionate hearing from behind bars, and the judge, whose own eyes were not immune to the earnest yearning of a father's love, made a pivotal decision.

In a surprising twist of grace, the judge overruled the previous order and granted the mother custody of her precious Aliyah once again. The ruling felt like divine intervention, a prayer answered, a family's love triumphing over the cold bureaucracy.

And so, Aliyah Faith Diaz returned to the embrace of her family. Her mother's tireless efforts and her father's whispered prayers across the sterile prison phone lines had navigated her back home - to the Lower East Side, or as the locals affectionately called it, the L.E.S.

Though life's tribulations didn't end there, and the road ahead was threaded with countless challenges, one truth stood strong as the backbone of Aliyah's life - she was no longer alone against the currents of the world. She stood surrounded by siblings who defended her, a mother who empowered her, and a father who, despite his absence, instilled in her a profound sense of

In her homecoming, Aliyah's heart, once tinged with the bruises of bullying, began to heal. For she knew the greatest lesson of all - that love is the truest form of resilience. And with each passing day, beneath the towering cityscape of the L.E.S., Aliyah Faith Diaz continued to weave her tale of triumph, one mathematical problem at a time.

A father return

In shadows deep and nights so hollow, A father's heart, once strong, now follows The path where sorrow weaves its nest, His soul aches for the test

Of battles fought with justice blind, For his dear children left behind.

By cruel fate and harsh decree, Torn from him, his legacy.

Upon the ground, his hopes lay shattered, His dreams of laughter, now scattered By the mother's act that rent the ties, Leaving naught but his desperate cries.

And in the courts, where balance sways,'Tis not his turn, nor his days, To hold his kin, to be their guide, The verdict cast, his hands were tied.

The matriarch, stern and unyielding, Whispers cold, her words concealing A barbed decree, a fateful line—

"You'll wait till eighteen's sign."

In the silence of his dimming light, He trudges through his longest night,

A specter of his former glee, A father robbed of his decree.Depression's weight grew day by day, Without his children's bright array.

A hollow man, he seemed condemned To suffer time, not comprehend

Then sprouted hope—a digital bloom—Across the void, dispelling gloom.

A chance encounter, fate's design, His daughter's page—a lifeline, fine..

Through pixels danced their hearts' reconnect,Forging bonds time could not affect.

A message sent, a message seen, A bridge across what might have been.

Reunion born from virtual thread,Joy and tears together shed.

Years may pass and distance taunt, But love prevails, its what they want.

From this reunion sweet and dear, Comes healing for the times unclear, A father's love, forever strong, Together now where they belong.

19

One voice

In the world of varied faces, Colors blend and interlace, A tapestry of human races,

Each one holds a unique grace.

Beneath the skin, we're all akin,Our hearts all beat to the same tin, A symphony of different tones, Together, we're never alone.

Anthems of unity we sing,

Acknowledging the pain that's been,

Every hue a story tells, In every pitch, our humanity dwells.

Let's not draw lines but erase,Celebrate each other's culture and base,

Strength is in the colors' blend, In every shade, we find a friend.

Eyes reflect a soul's deep story, More than black, it's shared glory, Hands of every shade reach out, In brotherhood, we erase doubt.

For colors are but just an art, It's character that plays the truest part, Together as humans, we stand proud,

Our harmony is sung aloud.

In a multihued world, we find The purest love for humankind, For in each shade, there is worth, In every color, we find our Earth.

So let's cherish every tone, For every culture is our own, In the spectrum, we see life's arc, Together, we illuminate the dark.

Respecting one another is key, and promoting a message of unity and harmony is what brings us all forward, regardless of our skin color or ethnic background.

Still my baby

In the dawn's soft whisper, where dreams gently sway, There's a name, dear Peanut, that starts my heart's day.Mama by affection, a sweet serenade,

Your voice is the music on life's grand parade.

Each morning is brighter with you as its muse, A symphony's prelude, an enchanting ruse.The world must bear witness, let them all align, To the love that proclaims, forever, "she's mine."

Awaiting the moment, 'neath a veil of white, I can't wait to marry, to bask in the light Of a love so enduring, my heart's daily bread Without your sweet cadence, my soul's underfed.

Each utterance of love, each "I love you" pledge,

To me, is as vital as the air we allege.

Completeness enfolds me, a life redefined;

In three words, a universe, our stars intertwined.

Oh, what I yearn most, with a longing so fierce, Is the spider-clasp embrace, none other coerces.When you leap into arms, legs securely entwined, It's the world in a hug, two hearts beat combined.

So Peanut, my Mama, till the end of our days, I'll cherish each instant, each loving phrase.For you are my constant, my grounding, my truth, My everyday wonder, my eternal youth.

The house of strangers

Once a man named John worked tirelessly, like an industrious bee, to provide for his large family - four of his own children and another four that came with the love of his life, Amanda. His voice often failed him when engaging with other women, but it never impeded his determination or his affection for his family. Sparing no effort, he amassed a small fortune and allowed himself the simple pleasure of a few toys - motorcycles that provided an escape from the tumult of a demanding life, and a new black on black Toyota RAV4 that he affectionately christened the "Night Ryder."

Life, as it is, traffics in the unexpected, and John's was no exception. A misstep, a moment's lapse hurled him behind the grim iron gates of a prison, leaving his home bereft of its patriarch... Amanda, though employed, was dancing a delicate tango with health issues that whispered promises of making her abandon her job - promises it kept before long

.

One desolate call from John's cold confines brought him news no father wants to hear - his stepson had crashed one of the cherished motorcycles, a machine that was supposed to be secured, its keys a treasure tucked away. The source of John's frustration was not only the totaled bike but the blatant disrespect for his property and efforts. The following week, John confronted his stepson with a stern but fair ultimatum, "You're grown, and responsibility is your shadow. You will repay me every dime of the $4500."

Time slithered by in his concrete cell, and the matter of the money, now a phantom subject, was skirted away into shadows until mentioned - sparking fury in Amanda. John reasoned, laying a portion of the blame at her feet, but as is his nature, he maintained a temperate demeanor. He tried to bridge the distance with letters and tender notes, only to be met with Amanda's claims of being confounded by their contents

With patience fraying, John broached another wound - the absence of Amanda's visits to his cell. His heart, already shackled, felt the added weight of abandonment. Then, one evening, a phone call bore the grim tidings that "Night Ryder" was no longer in the driveway; the SUV had been repossessed. Amanda's dismissal of the fees as extortionate tinged his thoughts with bitterness - perhaps she was relieved; she had never wanted the expense of the car to begin with.

John's life, which once revolved around the well-being of eight hearts that beat in his home, was now punctuated by the sterile clicks of a prison clock, and the silent acknowledgement that his world outside was fraying at the seams. The darkness of his cell matched the darkness that seemed to overshadow his family's life, yet he clung to hope that maybe, just perhaps, with time, hard work, and a little hustle of the heart - the pieces might come together once more.

Eric Dickerson

In a quiet street's embrace, where sunlight threads the leafy lace, There dwelt a youth, strong-willed and keen, by name, he's called Eric Dickerson.

From tender age through years amassed, his mother's love, a steadfast mast, She bore the weight of dual roles, seeding dreams in nurturing soils.

With dawn's first light to evening's dim, her strength, a song, a tireless hymn, A solo guardian in life's great dance, nurturing Eric's every chance.

Schooled in life's stern, hushing tones, he walked through halls of echoing stones, A mind alight with law's fair page, a heart unbound from societal cage.

At twenty-four, his tassel flipped, from scholarly seas, his vessel equipped, Certified in pre-law's stringent claim, against life's trials, a quenching flame.

Branded by times behind cold bars, he emerged with eyes fixed on the stars, For he sought to kindle hope's fierce fire, in troubled teens caught in the mire.

The courtroom loomed, a stage of fate, where truth and penance oft debate, He stood there poised, with contrite heart, longing for a brand new start.

"Your Honor," he began to say, "my past, I rue it every day,

Time wasted, lessons sharply learned, respect and wisdom, painfully earned."

"I stand before you, soul stripped bare, remorseful for the time and care, My mother's hours, her tireless aid, the sacrifices she has made.

For her, I strive to rise, to soar, to be the son she's yearning for, For every teen who's lost and scared, I vow my life to be paired."

To redirect their stormy plight, with empathy to curb their fight,

To guide them through each tempest tossed, to be their anchor, no matter the cost.

For in the tale of Eric Dickerson, a saga of hope has just begun, In tender youth, where whispers start, he echoes love, a mother's art.

So let the records show this day, a young man's will to pave the way, For each lost soul on life's harsh street, with Eric there, they'll find their feet.

With gratitude to courts and time, his mother's love—his mountain climb, For he is her unwavering light, a testament of love's true might.

My own kind of miracle

Once upon a time in the bustling neighborhoods of North Philadelphia, there lived a woman who, unfortunately, fell ill to a mysterious sickness. Confined by the limits of her malady, she felt the walls of her small apartment close in around her as the city buzzed with life beyond her reach.

Her name was Marjorie, and she was a kind soul, but the sickness that gripped her with feverish intensity brought forth a darkness from within her that she never knew existed. With each passing day of solitude, her frustration cankered into a rage that clawed at her sanity. The doctors were baffled, offering remedies that merely gnawed at the edges of her illness

.

One feverish night, as Marjorie tossed in her bed, soaked in sweat and anguish, a sinister thought crept into her mind like a whisper from the shadows. "Why should I suffer alone?" she mused, the bitterness corroding her once-gentle perspective.

When dawn broke, Marjorie embarked on a treacherous journey fueled by retribution, a deviant plan forming within her troubled mind. She would traverse from state to state, city to city, sharing her illness with as many unsuspecting souls as she encountered. It was as if the sickness itself was guiding her, whispering coordinates and infusing her with a perverted sense of purpose.

Armed with malice, she wandered the markets of North Philly, mingling with the crowds, her touch indiscriminate as she passed along her affliction. Strangers greeted her with open naivety, unaware of the invisible scourge she carried. Each handshake, each shared object, each conversation left in her wake was an opportunity to spread her pain.

In the quiet corners of Philly where community thrived, people began to show the same symptoms Marjorie had come to loathe.

The spread was slow at first, but as weeks turned into months, the sickness took root in homes and engulfed entire blocks.

Unrest began to bubble amongst the residents, with whispers of an epidemic. Unconnected by logic, yet irrevocably linked through Marjorie's shadowed acts, the community's health ebbed away while hospitals filled with the ill. Fear crept into the city's heart, gnawing at the collective conscience that something unnatural was afoot.

Marjorie, meanwhile, continued her deleterious pilgrimage. She was a wraith slipping through bus stations and hitching rides to reach new territories. And with each state line crossed, her legend grew, though no one yet connected the dots back to the lonely, embittered woman.

It was in a Midwestern town that Marjorie's journey met an abrupt end. Weakened by the very sickness she propagated, she collapsed in a diner's booth one stark morning. As they rushed to help her, the locals couldn't have known of the malevolent gift she had given them.

The sickness, however, began to ebb away from Marjorie as quickly as it had come, leaving her feeble but clear-minded in a sterile hospital room, resembling once again the kind-hearted woman she had been. Reports of the illness began to fade from the news, and cities slowly regained their vitality as the wave of sickness retracted, leaving behind a lesson in its wake.

Marjorie spent her days in recovery wrestling with the enormity of her actions, her anger now a distant echo overshadowed by remorse. In her heart, she knew no amount of penance could undo the sorrow she had caused. And though she was healed in body, the scars she left on towns and cities, and within her own spirit, remained a solemn testament to the price of her vengeance.

The story of the traveling illness became something of urban legend, a tale whispered in the wind that caressed the streets of North Philly—a reminder that sickness should be met with compassion, not contempt, lest it poison more than just the body.

A Love That Distance Can't Break

In a world confined by cold steel bars, A lonely heart echoes through prison halls, Yearning for a touch now distant as stars, His soul cries out, for his beloved it calls.

Shellz, O Shellz, my sweet absent grace, The warmth of your hand, the comfort it gave, Now lost to the void of this desolate place, In dreams alone, I'm no longer brave.

Each memory a treasure, a painful delight, Your laughter, a melody, now silent in air, Scrolling on your phone, that soft screen light, Gone, like whispers of wind in your hair.

Oh how I miss our dinner dates, the bustling scenes, The clatter of dishes, your smile across the table, A glass of wine, in the glow of city light beams, Fading now, into a fable that I am unable to label.

The mundane turned magic when you stood by my side, Even the supermarket aisles had tales to tell, Together, choosing delights we'd later on divide,

Now it's just the echo of my cell's hollow bell.

Shellz, I miss you, why won't you visit me?

Is the road too long, the barrier too high?

This concrete box, it binds, but my heart is free, And for a glimpse of you, it will forever try.

Until the day I emerge, when justice finds its time, Mi hold on to hope with every ounce of my might, For the loss of your presence - it's a steep climb, A relentless ache from morning to night.

But know, Shellz, my love, it knows no bounds, And it reaches for you, beyond these gray stones, Hoping for a reunion, where once again surrounds, The touch, the sight, and all the joyful tones.

His Harlem Flower

In Harlem, on the corner of dreams, 125th & Lex, Our paths crossed; it's a tale that complex Introduced by a figure from the street named Murda, Little did we know, our lives would stir a bit furdra.

You, with a presence, couldn't help but flaunt, While Murda's stunts made him the usual haunt.

But amidst the swagger, there you stood out, Surrounded by mystery, making me want to find out.

About what made you smile, what gave you blues, Your cherished dreams, your deeply held views.

From likes and dislikes, I wanted every detail,

Yet the path to your world seemed like a veiled trail.

Opportunity presented, sly as a furtive fox,

When I asked to borrow your pink Moto from Sprint, unorthodox.

Shyly dialing my number under an innocent guise, Handing it back, behind my eyes a plan lies

Later that night, when the city's hum was low, I broke the silence, a simple text to overthrow.

A message that sparked a conversation so bright, From that simple hello, it was up from that night.

Friendship, maybe love, started to swell, From borrowed moments a story to tell.

Harlem was the stage, the streets our narrative's core, Do you remember how we met? It's a tale to adore.

The Mending

In shadowed whispers, cells rebel,

A silent storm begins to swell, With rogue intention, stark and cruel, It breaks the

body's sacred rule.

A quiet mutiny inside,

Where mutant legions seek to hide, This thief of time, this stealthy blight,

Upon the body's sacred right.

Innocent in flesh, it breeds,

A scourge that festers, grows, and feeds, Cancer, vile usurper's name,

A life's match struck to a twisted flame.

Yet with every dawn there's hope, Against this spectral foe we cope, With science's sword, and courage's shield,We fight, we cry, we do not yield.

Warriors in white, their minds alight, Chase the cure with all their might, Through research's rigor, treatments grace,They race to help the ones they face.

Each soul, a story, strength within, A battle waged 'neath the skin, Survivors rise from ashes, soar,Emblems of the fights they've bore

.

To those we've lost, a reverent pause, Their lives gave meaning to the cause, In memory, their love still guides, As in our hearts, they still reside.

This enemy, with face unseen,

May shake our world, invade our dream, But human spirit, fierce and true, Shall rise to face the morning dew.

And so we stand, together, fast,

Believing each day could be the last, With love as beacon, hope as lance, We offer life another chance.

No malady can quell our song, For life is precious, life is long, And even in the darkest night, Well find a way to bring the light.

Forever a king

In the heart of Wakanda, beneath the mantled sky, A hero's tale is whispered, where the panther spirits lie.A king who walked among us, with a regal, silent stride, Chadwick Boseman, our Black Panther, filled with grace and pride.

A noble heart, a warrior's poise, With quiet strength, he carried the voice Of ancestors, and those yet to come, He spoke of unity, not kingdoms to be won.

On silver screens, he brought to life a dream, A utopia, where all is not as it seems, Where Vibranium shields and heritage thrives, In Wakanda, forever, his legacy survives.

With the salute,"Wakanda Forever" in his clasp,

He taught us love, and history in his grasp.

His battles fought, not just in fiction's frame, But in our world, against injustice and pain.

Chadwick, the man, with courage untold, Faced his own fight, with a spirit bold.

Never waning, through trials, unseen, A true superhero, not just on the screen.

He danced through the cosmos, king among stars, His light now guides us, from realms afar.A panther in the night, swift and wise,In the kingdom of memory, where his spirit never dies.

So, let us honor his journey, his irreplaceable role, For he was not just an actor, but a beacon—a soul.Look to the heavens, there, his essence does roam, In the heart of Wakanda, where he forever finds home.

Black Lives Matter

In every heart, a truth does ring, Black lives matter, let it sing.

Voices echo, far and wide,

Equal worth cannot be denied.

Shadows of history's pain we see, Generations cried, yearned to be free.

Their whispers in the wind still flow, Black lives matter, this we know.

Streets swell with countless feet, Marching as one to a freedom beat.

Chanting for change, they bravely stand, Demanding justice throughout the land.

Look upon the faces, rich with dreams, How often their hope tore at the seams.

Still, with vigor, their courage climbs, For black lives matter through the times.

No more should mothers shed their tears, For sons and daughters lost to fears.

Their names, a litany we raise, In their memory, our voices blaze.

For every life deemed less by shade, Is a blight upon humanity's grade.

Let us rise, unite, obliterate,

The ignorance that feeds the hate.

Equality, not just a word to say, A truth to live, the only way.

With strength to admit where we've failed, Together a fairer world unveiled.

So let us pledge, in love entwined, To honor every hue mankind.

For black lives matter, not just a phrase—A beacon of hope, through the haze.

Innocent behind the hood

In a world that judges by the cover, A hoodie clad, his fate discovered.

Color of night, but touch of fear, A black man's journey, harsh and sheer.

Innocent soul in casual wear, His story silenced in despair.

Fabric cast shadow on his skin, But underneath, life thins.Eyes cannot discern the heart, Yet swiftly tear his dreams apart.Labelled by a woven hood,Misunderstood in his neighborhood.

The trigger's call, so abrupt, A life ceased, so corrupt.

Echoes ripple through the night, Another star deprived of light.

A melanin-rich visage, a target found, Injustice rooted, deeply bound.For the color of his frame,

He bore the weight of centuries-old blame.

No crime committed, just a walk, Silent prayers in sidewalk chalk.A mother's tears, the world's amiss,

Her son taken by prejudice.

Are we naught but shades and tones?Reduced to skin, to blood, to bones?When will the world, unbiased, see, Beyond the hood, a man, just be?

In remembrance of countless lives, In hopes that true equality thrives.

Let not the color, nor the attire, Ignite baseless fear, provoke gunfire.A poem for the fallen, gone too soon, Underneath the unthreatening moon.For being merely who he was, An unwritten end, just because.

Black man, hoodie, existence ceased.

Pray one day this fear is released.

Until all can walk, no fear of attack, Be they clad in hoodie, white or blac

The green mile

In shadows cast on stone cold walls, An echo of time's grim protocol,

Where hope once bloomed, now finds its fall, And solitude's embrace is all.

Upon this death row, silent screams, Life hemmed by iron bars in seams, Each breath, a burden heavy weighs,

While empty hours turn to days.

The heart beats slow, the soul feels spent, For in this place, life's hues are bent, The taste of freedom, just a dream,

As fate unfolds its final scheme.

The condemned soul counts down in rue, What once was, nevermore anew,In whispered prayers, seeks mercy's touch, But knows the reaper's hand clutches much.

With every sun that rises, sets, The past a shroud of deep regrets, A tapestry of choices made, In twilight's grasp, all colors fade.

No hope to light the darkened hall, No pardon to interrupt the call, The final walk, a path alone, To answer for what can't atone.

The last meal, a ritual feast,

A somber prelude to the beast, That lurks beyond the chamber's door, Where breath and thought will dance no more.

In that still moment, all stands clear, The heartbeat's drum, the creeping fear,A silent plea for gentle fate,As the condemned meets the gate.

A flash, a moment, then it's done,The final setting of life's sun,

No hope to cling, no tears to shed, On death row, with the living dead.

Rhythms of the Night: The MR.CEO Odyssey

Prologue

The streets of Harlem, once echoing with the soulful rhythms of jazz and the fiery passion of hip-hop, now throbbed with a new beat. In the heart of this ever-evolving cultural mosaic, one man had risen above all, a party promoter known simply as MR. CEO. Empowered by a charm that could only be described as otherworldly, and a brand that was synonymous with the apex of nightlife—Pretty Boy Ent—MR.CEO had shaped the way people grooved under the city's shimmering lights.

Chapter 1

The Origin Beat

MR.CEO, born Darryl Jones, had come from humble beginnings. His early life in Harlem was a labyrinth of struggles and triumphs, all of which helped shape the resilience and savvy that would later define him. From the stoops of his neighborhood, he watched the world, taking in the raw rhythm of street life and internalizing it, letting it fuel his future dreams.

A natural leader with an impeccable sense of style, Marcus decided early on that he wanted to craft experiences that would leave people yearning for more—thus Pretty Boy Ent was born. He dreamt of bringing together individuals from all walks of life to celebrate the unifying power of music, dance, and community. His weapon of choice? Parties that resonated with the heartbeats of his patrons.

Chapter 2

The Labyrinth of the Night

House parties were just the beginning. His events, initially confined to the friendly confines of residential rooftops and lofts, soon outgrew their walls and tumbled into the streets and clubs of Harlem. But Marcus was not satisfied with just any party—he wanted his events to be transcendent, transformative. This led him to the less-charted territories—underground gatherings that became the stuff of legends.

Whispers of Pretty Boy Ent's events spread like wildfire, their reputations built on the promise of an unimaginable escape from reality. And MR.CEO delivered. Each affair was meticulously crafted, from the enigmatic entryways leading to pulsing dance floors to the carefully curated playlists echoing from the hands of the city's most underground DJs.

Chapter 3

The Literary Turntable

Fame, as it does, evolved MR. CEO's aspirations. The man of the night, the legend of Harlem's party scene, found solace and a new calling in the quiet realm of words. Now a budding author, he channeled the electric energy of his parties into the written word, crafting stories that echoed the vibrancy and vicissitudes of the lives he once united in celebration.

With two books on the cusp of publication, Darryl found another unexpected partnership in the Bottega Boyz, a crew of influencers and tastemakers. Their combined vision: to merge the literary world with the ephemeral magic of events—an intersection of storytelling and experiential vibrance.

Chapter 4

The Homecoming Crescendo

Now, as MR. CEO stood on the brink of a grand homecoming, the streets of Harlem buzzed with anticipation. Far from the raucous promoter of the past, MR.CEO was an amalgam—a party legend turned reflective author, an alchemist of moments and memories.

His plans were grander than ever. With book launches masquerading as rapturous events, Darryl was set to infuse his literary offerings with the very essence of the parties for which he was revered. It was more than a comeback; it was a renaissance, a reinvention of the MR.CEO brand that would ripple through the cultural fabric of Harlem and beyond

Epilogue

As the city that never sleeps braced for the unfolding tapestry of MR.CEO's latest chapter, Darryl stood at his favorite spot

How he holds his head

In crowns of coils, each twist and turn, Lies a legacy, deep, profound

A lineage of strength, a history earned, In every lock, ancestors resound.

Black is the night, vast and bold, A canvas endless, from which stars are told.

It's the hue of resilience, of stories untold, Of dreams wrapped in night's protective fold.

Those locks, they whisper tales of old, Of struggles, victories, spirits like gold They speak of pride, of beauty, uncontrolled, A testament to a culture brave and bold.

To be black, to have locks, is to hold A universe within, diverse and manifold.

It's unity, community, a hand to uphold, A journey through time, forever enrolled.

To wear them is to defy, to be unenrolled From standards imposed, from molds.It's a statement, a stance, courageously scrolled, An ode to freedom, in every fold.

In every kink, every curl, every braid,

Lie echoes of songs through hardships wade.

A collective power that will never fade, Armor of heritage, uniquely made.From the roots of Africa's rich soil,

To the bustling streets of modern toil, Locks carry the blood, the sweat, the turmoil, Yet also the joy, the grace, the spoils.

To be black with locks, is to proudly declare, An identity strong, and beyond compare.

A culture, a memory, a soul laid bare, A life lived with intention, love, and care.

So let these locks flow, free and long, A symbol of a

people, ageless and strong.

In them is a story, a perpetual song, Of what it means to be black and belong.

Harlem to Here

Yo...
Harlem raised a boy named holiday who
Ran with Danny, with Damien, and Janiqua fine.they went to p.s.169
Block dreams heavy, hearts light as the air,
Two dudes liked her, but he ain't never share.
He held it in quiet, that crush on the low,
Before he could tell her, life said, "You gotta go."
Group home walls, letters bleeding from his pen,
Sent 'em all to Janiqua, but she never wrote again.
He came back home, went knocking her door,
Her momma just said, "She don't live here no more."
He asked and he asked, but the answer stayed the same,
Left him standing in silence with the weight of her name.
Years went by, but the flame never died,
He built up his life, but the hurt stayed inside.
Then fate came around, like it knew where to land,
She'd been living in his state—right there, close at hand.
All that time gone, all those nights he would miss,
Dreaming of a chance, now it feels like this—
Like life gave him back what the streets took away,
Like Janiqua was meant to still hear what he say.
So he stands as a man, no longer that kid,
Ready to tell her the truth that he hid.
Harlem to here, the circle complete,
When love never leaves, it's just waiting to meet.

I WANNA FUCK THE SHIT OUTTA YOU!

I WANNA FUCK THE SHIT OUTTA YOU!

NOT make love
Fuck being gentle!
Fuck all that romance for your mental!
I WANNA FUCK THE SHIT OUTTA YOU!
Like ah hoe on da strip do
Fuck bein' nice!
fuck the entice!
Fuck turnin' off the lights!
Suck you dry
Slap your thighs
Bite you ass with no class
Stick my hand in your pussy while you gasp
Lick on dat clit til' you blast!
I WANNA FUCK THE SHIT OUTTA YOU!
Like I'm your pimp and you dead broke
Bang your head on the bed post
Til' your body and your hair soak
Fuck you up against the wall
Fuck your ass on the ground
watch you try to crawl away from this pound after pound!
I WANNA FUCK THE SHIT OUTTA YOU!
Til' you go into convulsion's
No emotion in my motion's
No foreplay, Massage or lotions
Just sweat, cum and lust
Just thrust after thrust!
Til I cus' and I scream and my nut starts to bust!
I JUST FUCKED THE SHIT OUTTA

Bottega Boy Dee

Three years in the Feds, silence in the mail,
Little to no letters, but I never let it frail.
Ten toes planted, I stood on my ground,
No crowd, no clique, just me holding it down.
While others walked in packs, I chose to move dolo,
A soldier in my lane, writing life's solo.
No mold can contain me, no hand can define,
I'm the author of my grind, this story is mine.
I came home hungry, pavement under feet,
Running to the bag, chasing what's concrete.
No chains on my spirit, no leash on my plan,
I'm independent, hard working, a self-made man.
Through cold nights and trials, I carried my name,
Bottega Boy Dee — I'm built from the flame.
Not cocky, just steady, the real in my chest,
I survived, I prevailed, and I'm built for success

Janiqua, the One Who Stayed in His Heart

In Harlem he walked, where the brownstones rise,
A boy with a dream and a fire in his eyes.
At P.S. 169, the days felt so free,
Running with Danny, with Damien, with she.
Janiqua—her name was a song in his mind,
A beauty, a light, one of a kind.
He carried a crush, though Damien did too,
Two hearts in secret, but only she knew.
Then life took a turn, sent him far from the block,
To a group home of rules, of chains, and of locks.
He wrote her in ink, his soul on each line,
But silence returned, not a word, not a sign.
When at last he came back, he ran to her place,
Hoping for comfort, to see her sweet face.
Her mother just said, "She don't live here no more,"
And with each cold repeat, his heart hit the floor.
Years rolled ahead like the wheels of a train,
He carried the question, the ache, and the pain.
Until fate was kind, showed its hand once again—
She'd lived in his state all along, just the same.
No distance of oceans, no borders, no miles,
Just missed opportunities stacked in the piles.
And now as a man, he can start where he should,
To love her with patience, with fire, with good.
For some stories bend, but they never quite break,
And some hearts hold on for however long it takes.

Harlem Boy and Janiqua

He was born in Harlem, where the sidewalks breathe,
Where kids played ball and wore hearts on their sleeves.
At P.S. 169, he found his first crew,
Danny, and Damien, and Janiqua too.
They laughed through the summers, they walked through the cold,
Dreams in their pockets, too heavy to hold.
But the boy kept a secret, a flame he would hide,
A crush on Janiqua that burned deep inside.
Damien felt it too, the same pull, the same fire,
But neither could silence that quiet desire.
And before he could speak it, life turned him around,
A group home would take him far from their ground.
He sat with his pen in the still of the night,
Pouring his soul out in letters he'd write.
Page after page, he confessed what he felt,
Praying her hands would unfold what he dealt.
But weeks turned to months, and months into years,
No answers came back, only silence and tears.
When at last he came home, with hope in his chest,
He went to her doorstep, his heart put to test.
Her mother stood steady, her face held no clue,
"She don't live here," was all she would do.
He begged for an answer, a hint, or a sign,
But the words stayed the same, like a clock stuck in time.
So he carried the ache, and he carried the name,
Through the struggle of years, through hardship and pain.
Life made him harder, but deep in his soul,
The thought of Janiqua still made him whole.
Then one twist of fate, when the years had grown long,
Revealed she'd been near him, not vanished, not gone.
The same state, the same skies, the same city air—
All that time wasted, and she had been there.
Now older, now wiser, the boy turned a man,

He saw a new chance, and he formed a new plan.
To not waste the moments, to not let it slide,
To tell her the truth he once buried inside.
For some loves don't fade, they just wait in the dark,
And some names are carved on the soul like a mark.
Janiqua—the one he had lost, yet still found,
A circle completed, the world spinning round.
And maybe this time, the letters will land,
Delivered by fate, carried hand into hand.
For Harlem once raised him, but love made him stay,
And Janiqua still shines in his heart to this day.

Thoughts of an inmate

In the valley low, 'neath the hilly crest, A man returned from a quest for rest.
His heart encased in a weathered shell, From years confined in a prison cell.
No crime too great had this man done, Just took a wrong turn, fate's cruel pun.
He longed for warmth, for a fresh new start, To kindle hope in a kindred heart.
Upon the hilly slopes so green and fair, He met a woman with midnight hair.
Eyes that held the depth of night, Yet flinched from love, from the gentlest light.
Her spirit wounded, trust all but spent, By hands unkind and words that bent.
The beauty of her soul, those hills concealed,Behind walls built not to yield.
This man, once caged, now free to roam, Sought not just freedom, but a home.
A place to dwell, a hand to hold, A story of redemption to be told.
With gifts of laughter, little charms, He tried to pierce her cold alarms.
No grand gestures could unfurl The wary heart of this guarded girl.
With patience like the mountain stream, He wove respect into his dream.
Not with haste, but with a quiet plea, He showed her what it means to be free.
"Let's mend, not break," so softly spoken, A promise made, a token unbroken.
Through seasons of silence, and misty rain, He proved that love could bloom from pain.
But the heart, once scorned, stays ever wary, For the past can make the present scary.
Despite his trials to bridge that moat, Like petals in the wind, his efforts float.
The man who wore the shackle's weight, Learned that some locks have no key of fate.
Her heart remained a fortress strong, And he, outside, where he belonged.
Yet still he stays, in sight of her hill, A testament to his unwavering will.
Perhaps one day, her pain will part, And let in the man who earned her heart.

The Boy from Harlem and Janiqua

He grew up in Harlem, on streets alive with sound,
At P.S. 169, where his roots were first found.
Running with Danny, with Damien too,
And Janiqua, the girl who made skies turn blue.
Both he and Damien felt sparks in their chest,
But he held it quiet, kept his heart suppressed.
Then fate drew a line—he was sent far away,
To a group home where nights turned to letters each day.
He wrote to Janiqua, poured truth on the page,
Hoping his words might cross distance, not age.
But silence returned, unanswered, unheard,
No trace of her laughter, no comfort, no word.
When freedom came back, he ran to her door,
Her mother stood silent, repeating once more:
"She don't live here," was all she would say,
And the boy turned a man, had to walk away.
Years stacked on years, like bricks in the rain,
Memories faded, but the heart held the name.
Until one day, as destiny planned,
He found she'd been near, in the very same land.
Not oceans apart, not cities away,
But living beside him, through year after day.
And so he began, where the story had paused,
A chance to rewrite all the time

The Unrequited Obsession

In the bustling city of New Angeles, there was a renowned gynecologist named Dr. Julian Crest, whose expertise and compassionate demeanor had earned him the respect and adoration of his patients. Among them was a woman named Elara Simmons, whose routine check-up marked the beginning of an intense infatuation that soon spiraled out of control.

Elara, a graphic designer by profession, had never given much thought to love or romance, consumed by her career and personal projects. However, her encounter with Dr. Crest shattered her focus.

He was not only exceptionally skilled but also exuded a warmth and kindness that left a deep impression on her. The more she thought about her appointment, the more entranced she became with her doctor. It was not long before infatuation took root in Elara's heart, and she convinced herself that Dr. Crest was her soulmate.

As weeks passed, Elara's affection grew into an obsession. She began to construct a fantasy world where she and Dr. Crest were destined to be together. In her mind, their brief professional interactions were imbued with hidden romantic meanings, and she hung onto his every word as if they were personal declarations of love.

Elara's behavior started to change. She found herself driving by the clinic on her way to work, conjuring up excuses to schedule unnecessary appointments, and even sending Dr. Crest gifts and letters that were more personal than appropriate. The situation escalated when

Elara, unable to accept the lack of reciprocation, intensified her pursuit.She began to follow Dr. Crest, learning his routines, his hangouts, and even his favorite coffee shop. Her presence became a constant shadow in his daily life, uninvited and persistent. She would wait for him to finish work, longing for a chance to'accidentally' run into him. Social media was her ally in tracking his interests and whereabouts, fueling her misguided conviction that they shared a special connection that only she could see.

Dr. Crest initially dismissed the signs as harmless admiration, but Elara's persistence soon started to concern him. When strange coincidences turned into undeniable patterns, he felt his privacy being violated. He became wary of the overbearing attention, and it dawned on him that his patient's behavior was no longer simply eccentric-it was dangerous.

As Elara's overtures grew more desperate, Dr. Crest took necessary precautions, including talking to Elara about professional boundaries and having a frank conversation about the inappropriate nature of her actions. When this approach failed to deter her, he was forced to involve security at the clinic and consider legal action to ensure his safety and the safety of his staff

The mayhem in Dr. Crest's life reached its peak when Elara made an unexpected scene at a medical conference he was attending, declaring her love for him in front of his colleagues. It was painfully clear that her perception of reality had been distorted by her obsession.

With a heavy heart, Dr. Crest sought a restraining order, and Elara was compelled to receive psychological help. The process of healing was long and arduous for both of them. For Elara, it was coming to terms with the false narrative she had built, and for Dr. Crest, it was regaining the feeling of safety and normalcy in his life.

In the end, the story of Elara Simmons served as a cautionary tale about the fine line between love and obsession, and the importance of recognizing when admiration crosses over into the territory of compulsion. For the beauty of love lies not in its fervor but in its mutual embrace, and without it, affection can warp into something tragic and consuming.

Breonna Taylor

In the quiet of the night, she lay in restful sleep, Breonna Taylor, a life so full, a dream so deep.

A healer by day, she tended with care, Never knowing that night would be laced with despair.

The shuffle of feet, the shattering breach, A storm of confusion, no time for speech.

In the sanctity of home, where love should have been,

Echoed the clamor of a world so grim.

Uniformed shadows danced through the halls, Blind bullets spoke in deadly calls.

A life snuffed out, without a chance to fight, A candle extinguished, in the grasp of the night.

"Say her name," the people cry, For justice and peace, we cannot deny.

Breonna Taylor, who under her roof, Became a symbol, an undeniable truth.

Her spirit now marches in the hearts of the throng, Her name a chorus, a powerful song.

No more the silence, no more the night, For in her memory, we'll stand for what's right.

A daughter, a sister, a healer, a friend, May your legacy, Breonna, never see its end.

In the quest for equality, your story we tell, And in the gardens of justice, may your memory dwell.

When shadow lift they disappear

In a bustling town, a man once stood tall, Known by so many, beloved by all, His name on the lips of folk near and far, As radiant and constant as the northern star.

A friend to the masses, a face in the crowd, His laughter was music, hearty and loud.

A giver of time, a sharer of tales, His life, a ship, with billowing sails.

But winds do change, and storms arise,

The man's bright day met with darkened skies.

Through one cruel twist, locked away, confined, His freedom stripped, with his hands entwined.

Behind cold bars, away from the throng, He waited for signs he still belonged.

No footfalls echoed, no letters came,

Just silence, for him, and for them, no blame.

A haunting solitude, a heart's lament, For a bond, he thought, was robustly cement.

But alone he sat, in the dimming light,

No faces of old to ease his plight.

They say you learn in times quite dire,

Who'll stand with you when you tread through fire.

Yet the man in his cell, with a pain so grim, Learned a harsh lesson, on a waning whim.

For memories fade, and loyalties drift, And the ties that bind can sometimes shift.

A man who once knew people by scores, Now knows the echo of his own remorse.

So, take heed from the man whose circle was vast, And treasure the few whose love will truly last.

For not every soul that cheers in your prime, Will walk the hard miles through the tough climes.

Remember him there, in the quiet gloom, A lesson learned, in that lonely room.

For those who seem near when fortunes are sweet,

May vanish when adversity they meet.

A different kind of time

In towers of steel, the city's might, A man paces his 9 to 5 plight.

Each day he greets the morning throng, Each heartbeat marching to labor's song.

With every tick of the solemn clock, His hands embrace the routine lock.

Fingers dance on keys, numbers blend, Working, earning, to meet each end.

Daylight trades for fluorescent sung, While dreams hang silent,
on his tongue.

A cog in the wheel, feeling every spin, The echo of his labor, a ceaseless din.

But life, it turned on a fickle dime, Led him astray, to a darker time.

Where mistakes were made, heavy costs, In freedom's loss, his life was tossed.

Behind cold bars, the mighty fall, From towering wage to echoing call.

A shadow now, where once was a man, Whose hours are counted on a different plan.

Now making money, a pittance it seems, Measured in cents, not in dreams.

Each coin a clang in the federal jar, Each day blurring, each
scar upon scar.

Between metal and stone, his spirit bends, But hope, resilient, never ends.

For even in depths, where daylight is spent, There's a flicker of faith, no cage can dent.

A man once clad in suit and tie, Now counts the stars in the penitent sky.

Though locked away, his heart's still free, A 9 to 5 man, changing his destiny.

Hope whispers soft, beneath the moon's glow, A chance for redemption, a new path to know.

For life's not over when one mistake screams, In the quiet of night, one can still dream.

Prisoners map

In walls of grey, where shadows play, And time drips slow, with dread array, A soul confined, with thoughts astray, Beneath the burden, heavy fray.

Oh, whispers call from freedom's light, Yet here I'm bound, far from the night, Each bar a sentence, each lock a blight, In my own thoughts, I fight the fight.

The pain within, a silent mate, It grips my heart, a cruel fate,

To know the weight of unseen hate, As bars of steel dictate my state.

Understanding pain, a hidden art, It's more than tears, it's life apart, From love, from joy, from morning's start, A chapter penned without my part.

For in this cell, my world's so small, Where echoes bounce, off

cold, hard wall, I ponder loss, and stand tall,

Embracing pain that comes to call.

Locked up in sorrow's tight embrace, I search for strength, a saving grace, And though confined, I seek a place, Where hope can bloom, in this dark space.

With each deep breath, I forge a key, To unlock wisdom, set pain free,Understanding grows, like a sturdy tree, Bearing fruit for the mind, resilience the bee.

Locked away, but not alone,

In pain's harsh school, where I've been shown, The power of endurance, of love's backbone, In suffering's depths, compassion has grown.

So while these walls may hold me tight, My spirit dances far from sight, To a world beyond, where hearts unite, And understanding pain can turn to light.

Philly Still PA

I'm sick of the flex,
sick of the front,
folks from Philly actin' like
they somethin' different, on a hunt.
Ask 'em where they from,
they don't say the state,
they say "Philly," like the rest of PA
ain't hold no weight.
Now they handin' out city I.D.s,
like Philly stand alone,
but if you ain't got a state I.D.,
what's the point of callin' home?
Listen—
Pittsburgh to the Poconos,
Erie to the farms,
the Keystone hold it all together,
not just bells and rowhouse charms.
Yeah, Philly shine bright,
history deep, culture raw,
but without Pennsylvania
you ain't standin' tall.
So say it with your chest,
don't get lost in the haze—
you Philly, yeah, no doubt,
but you Pennsylvania always.

Confessions of a friend

In the realm of connection, beyond the hearts pure sway, Lies a bond quite different, in shades of night and day.

There with the taste of friendship, sweet and ever so light, Lurk whispers of desire, veiled in the cloak of night.

Beneath the guise of laughter, and shared, innocuous grins, Pulses surge clandestine, as subtle yearning begins.

A venture bold, unspoken, where emotions lie in wait, Two friends embark on a path, to a tempting, furtive state.

In the glow of moon's soft luminescence, secrets are shared, Where the currency of touch, is the only fare that's dared.

Entangled in a dance of need, where pleasure's the only end, Two souls seek solace and release, in the arms of a friend.

No promise of tomorrow, in this fleeting, tender game, They find solace in the silence, that speaks each other's name.

With the morning's light, they return to the chaste day's light, Yet know when dusk embraces, again they'll unite in the night.

But oh, tread cautiously, dear hearts, who mingle flesh with fun, For the weaving of such webs can be easily undone.

The heart, a fragile traveler, might find a hopeful dream, In the maze of 'benefits,' things are not all as they seem.

To seek warmth in another, without the binds of love, Requires understanding, and respect thereof.

May joy be found in moments, in caresses, sweet and briet, Yet remember, with the pleasure, sometimes comes the grief.

So here's to friends with secrets, in the dance of push and pull, May they navigate their passion, with a heart that's wise and full.

May the fun remain unfettered, as they respect the rules they set, In the game of friends with benefits, where friendship's the safe bet.

The writing on the wall

In the quiet realm where ideas soar high, Lies a warrior wielding not sword, but a sigh.

Gone are the days of clashing steel in hand, For battles are won on a much grander strand.

I need not brawl with fists of mortal flesh, Nor forge my victories in a tangle of mesh;

My words cut sharper than the bladed grass, Taming the fiercest pron with each poised pass.

With pen as my lance, I carve through the air, Each stroke on the page striketh true and fair.

The ink flows like blood from ancient duels, But heals, not wounds, as wisdom's precious jewels.

A syllable, a sentence, the gentlest of pleas, Can topple the might of a thousand decrees.

For in the world of thoughts, where silence roars, A poet commands and the universe soars.

Fierce debates roar like tempests unplanned, Yet fall serene to my script's gentle hand.

A word, just a whisper, can rend or repair,

Rendering armors of hatred to mere vaporware.

So behold my power, not of muscle or might, But of eloquent visions, and insight's bright light.

I speak, | write, I cast my decree, And set forth a future where minds are free.

No need for clashing, no need for fight,

When hearts can be conquered by the pen's sleek flight.

A transcendence from violence, a higher accord, Won by the might of the word, not the sword.

When best friends bloom

In the garden of life, where truths bloom and thrive, There lies a gem, more precious than gold in a hive.

It stands not in grandeur, nor seeks the limelight, A bond unbreakable, firm, holding hearts tight.

True friendship, a tapestry woven with trust, A mosaic of memories, a shield against gust.

Two souls in a dance, a balance so rare, Harmony and acceptance filling the air.

Not a fair-weather journey, but one that endures, Through tempests and droughts, its foundation secures.

A mirror of honesty reflecting your soul, Revealing your flaws but making you whole.

Whispers of laughter, secrets shared in hushed tones, Silences heavy, yet light as the stones.

Shoulders to lean on, when life seems too tough, Hands that hold tightly when the waters are rough. A friendship like this knows no bounds, no end, Not just a companion, but a true, steadfast friend.A lighthouse that guides through the fog and the mist, A warmth that remains in the cold, frost-kissed.

No race or creed can its power confine, For true friendship is ageless, borderless, divine.

It's the treasure within the clutter of life, A calming melody amidst the strife.

In this fast-paced world of fleeting relations, True friendship's a jewel of unwavering foundations.

A bond, a love that time cannot fray, A light that brightens even the darkest day.

So here's to the true friends who stand by our side, In their presence, our joys and sorrows collide.

May we cherish this gift, this rare form of art, For a true friendship is life's greatest chart.

When the locks loosen

In concrete halls of silence deep,

Where shadows cast and sorrows weep, A soul once bound, in patience steeped,Envisions now the light of keep.

Chains of past, with time, grow weak, Walls of iron, guard no more the meek, My jail time wanes, no longer bleak, I stand before freedom's peak.

Through the bars, a glimmer breaks, A hope that stirs, as dawn awakes, Each day a step that freedom makes, To life anew, no matter what it takes.

The echo of a closing door, Resounds a promise forevermore,

That binds of old need tighten no more,As I prepare to soar.

Almost over, this sentence cast,A journey through the shadows vast, To emerge unscathed from the tempest passed, With lessons learned, held steadfast.

The light of freedom calls me near, A beacon through the last of fear, A call to step into the clear, And leave behind each fallen Tear ? MmMy heart beats to a new found rhythm, Released from yesterday's darkened prism,I move ahead with optimism, To embrace life's endless spectrum.

So here I stand, at the threshold wide, With gratitude that cannot hide, For every moment, I've survived, And for the light where future abides.

The last last bell

In the quiet halls of learning,

Where young minds should thrive and grow, A shadow falls, hearts churning,Where once light was all we'd know.

Hush now, whispers in the locker rows, Echoes of a childhood song, Now disrupted by the throes

Of a tragedy so profound and wrong.

Books and pencils strewn aside, Laughter silenced in a flash, Dreams and innocence collide, Against a violent, hateful clash.

Empty desks, a mournful sight,Future stories left untold,

Bright aspirations snuffed by night, Young ambitions turned to cold.

A community in disarray,Faces streaked with endless tears, For the lives lost on that day, And the laughter no one hears.

Why must the halls of scholarsBecome the battlegrounds of fear?Why must we fail to collar The demons that draw near?

Oh, let us seek the wisdom, The courage to embrace peace, To prevent these darkened kingdoms And let such horrors cease.

May we rise above with action, With compassion in our view, To honor each lost fraction Of the lives we once knew.

Our hearts in unity, we mourn Each precious soul departed,

Determined that from sorrow born, No more shall the hopeful-hearted

Fall in the classrooms of our lands, Where instead love should be schooled,Where together we should stand And proclaim such acts are cruel.

In the quiet halls of learning, Let's vow to change the story, To kindle hope's bright burning, And restore them back to glory.

Stone walls and shattered truth

In the still of my cold, gray cell, My heart's truth, I yearn to tell, To friends and love I thought so dear, My voice, it seems, they do not hear.

With ink, my solemn words unfold,Beneath the bars where sorrows hold, I penned my need, quite clear and plain, Awaiting

warmth to ease my pain.

My so-called friend, where have you gone?

In my bleak hours, before the dawn, I asked you for a simple sum, To lighten days that have become- -

A stretch of silence, thick and grave,

No sign of the support | crave, The money for a visitor's chair, A plea for comfort in despair.

My so-called girl, our love once bright, Now shadows haunt our tender night.Each unmet call, a bitter sting, A crescendo of hope withering

.

Your silence breeds a deeper jail, Beyond the bars, my spirits fail.The echoes of my pleas return,Unanswered, as my insides churn.

Betrayal's embrace is tight and cold, Of empty promises once boldly told, Left with the ghost of your absence, A caricature of past pretense.

So here I sit in pondered thought, Lessons hard through hardship taught.The ring of truth, distinct and clear:

Support, like ghosts, just disappear.

In the company of four stark walls, The heart grows quiet, as hope befalls..For in this jail of both stone and pain, I've learned—some friendships are in vain.

Stop please don’t shoot

In the heart of the night, a plea rises clear, Echoing in the alleys where the shadows peer,"Stop, please don't shoot!" a desperate cry, Begging for mercy under the gunmetal sky.

Born from fear, where innocence bleeds, A chord of humanity frantically pleads.One voice, one demand, so raw and so brash, Clamoring for life in the split second's flash.

Gun in hand, power surges in veins, A moment of choice where only fear reigns."Stop, please don't shoot!" implores the air, A future hangs trembling in the crosshairs.In a world where violence seeks to rule, Compassion's whisper is a powerful tool.

Against the noise of hatred and dispute, Resounds the charge - "Stop, please don't shoot!"Might we listen before it's too late,

To the stifled cries beneath anger's weightFor the sound of peace is a simple flute, Playing its refrain:

"Stop, please don't shoot."

Hearts pounding loudly, time slows its race, A call for reason in a darkened space.

Life's fabric so thin, easily torn and moot,

Mend it with words,

"Stop, please don't shoot."

May wisdom prevail, may we find a way, To sheath our weapons, to let love sway.

So lift up your voices, don't let them be mute, Echo together,

"Stop, please don't shoot."

For in the anthem of the living, were all a note, In the symphony of survival, we all vote.

In harmonious chorus, our fears refute,

Arms laying down to the plea,

"Stop, please don't shoot!"

Thru the veins of grief

Beneath the skies of soft twilight dew, My heart still speaks, it calls for you, A bond unbroken by earth's farewell, In whispered winds, your stories dwell.

You clothed me in love's tender thread, Wove dreams into my days, it spread Through every memory, laugh, and tear, Your voice, a lullaby, I long to hear.

Oh, Mother mine, your fight was brave, Through pain and trials, you rode each wave.

You were the warrior, fierce yet kind, A light unyielding, in darkness shined

Your name upon my trembling lips,

Each sentence paused by sorrow's grips, I need to tell you all about The days you've missed since you stepped out.

The baby boy you left behind,

Now walks the path you've surely signed, Incomplete, a jigsaw piece astray, For part of me, with you, did lay.

In moments when the silence grows, That's when my yearning for you shows.I need to feel your presence near, To guide me through each passing year.

Though cancer took you from my side, It cannot steal the love inside, A river flowing without end,A broken heart, time cannot mend.

I speak to stars, they flicker bright,"Heaven stole my guiding light,"And yet I trust, beyond blue skies, Our souls converse, in love's reprise.

I seek you in the morning's hue, In every sunset kissed with dew, A part of you, in all I see, Baby girl, you're here with me.

So rest, my angel, free from pain,

Until the day we meet again, Within my heart, your laughter stays, I am yours, in countless ways.

The writer in the room

In Harlem's vibrant avenues, 'neath soaring city spires, There walked a man with pen in hand, igniting dormant fires.

Mr. CEO, they called him, a name that whispered power, A scribe turned magnate, clad in suits for the office's finest hour.

He penned his lore on bygone days, his words like silk did weave, Through urban sprawls and twilight's call, in what we call conceive.Yet life, it pitched a different plan, a venture of contrast, From the realm of ink and paper to a future vast and vast.

The echoes of his writer's soul, silenced by the climb, Through boardroom battles, stocks and charts, surrendering to time.

His stories lay in quiet repose, his muse put to the back, As CEO, he soared on highs but the writer's touch did lack.

The city watched this man ascend, a titan in its frame, Yet within him brewed a silent storm, a slowly rising flame.

Words, once dormant, stirred anew in whispered inner speech, For the scribe within can never die, though distant it may reach.

Now shadows flicker 'cross his desk, the corporate leap behind, Harlem's son with a gilded pen, a new chapter to unwind.

No longer back, but at the fore, his narrative's embrace, Mr. CEO, the writer, takes his rightful, storied place.

With wisdom gleaned from towers tall and streets that taught him grit, Each sentence bears a truth hard-won, each paragraph a hit.A comeback carved of dreams reborn, where once there was a cost, Harlem's bard in business cloaked, but never truly lost.

The city hums, a symphony for this man in his prime, Harlem roots and boardroom fruits, both harmonized in rhyme.

Mr. CEO, oh, what tales your resurgence will bestow, For in the heart of every word, you'll reignite your glow.

Philly Ain't Its Own World

Man, I'm sick of what I'm seein',
folks from Philly frontin' bold,
actin' like they not Pennsylvania,
like the story ain't been told.
Now they talkin' city I.D.s,
like Philly stand alone,
but if you rip the map apart,
where's the state you callin' home?
What's the point of Harrisburg,
what's the point of state pride,
if Philly carves its own lane,
like the rest just stepped aside?
It's Keystone through and through,
from the mountains to the streets,
don't matter if it's cheesesteaks,
or the land of Amish beats.
So yeah, you Philly, no denying,
but don't forget the line is drawn—
you still part of Pennsylvania,
always was, and still belong.

Philly Ain't Whole State pt. 2

Ask somebody where they from,
they don't stall, they don't wait,
they say "Philly all day,"
never "Pennsylvania State."
It's North, it's South, it's West,
it's the city that they claim,
from the block to the skyline,
every hood know the name.
But beyond that turnpike,
past the SEPTA line's end,
is farmland, small towns,
where the state still extends.
Pittsburgh got its steel,
Hershey got its sweet,
but Philly got the struggle
and the pride in every street.
Yeah, Pennsylvania holds it,
Philly just the crown,
but when you say you from the city,
they already know the sound.
So call it what you want,
rep the city, rep the state,
Philly's part of Pennsylvania—
but it move at its own rate.

Philly Ain't the Whole Map

When you ask, "Where you from?"
they don't pause, don't play,
they answer quick: "Philly."
not "Pennsylvania" today.
Chestnut Street, Broad Street,
cheesesteaks on the grill,
they wear it like a tattoo,
reppin' Philly with a thrill.
But Pennsylvania's bigger,
from Pittsburgh to the Poconos,
from Amish barns and farmland,
to steel towns where the river flows.
Philly's still a chapter
in the Keystone state's wide book,
but the city stands so mighty
it's the first thing people look.
So remember, when they tell you,
"I'm from Philly, that's my land,"
it's still Pennsylvania—
but Philly's what they understand.
A corner of the commonwealth,
yet its own bold design,
Philly ain't the whole state—
but it's a state of mind.

Juneteenth

Beneath the June sun's fervent heat, There lies a day we hold so sweet, Juneteenth—freedom's heart does beat,A history that's far from neat.

On Galveston's fair island shore, Arrived the news two years afore,A general with tidings bore, That slavery would be no more.

Emancipation's breath so deep, Awaked a people long asleep,

From heavy chains that caused to weep, They leaped with joy, no more to creep.

The nineteenth day of June we raise, A song of both the blues and praise, For ancestors with stoic gaze, Who fought for freedom's righteous ways.

In festive voice, we now narrate, A past which we cannot negate, The struggle for a fairer state, Where justice does not come too late.

Juneteenth stands for such a quest,

For true equality and rest,

Where all are free to live their best, And every soul is truly blessed.

We gather now in jubilee, And look upon history's tree, Its roots deep in harsh tyranny, Its fruits now ripe with liberty.

Let barbecue and music blare, Let dancing feet dismiss all care,

Let stories weave through evening air, And freedom ring out everywhere.

A tale of shackles broke apart,

A dream that's etched within the heart, Juneteenth, now a sacred art,Expresses where new starts embark.

So let us honor this great day, With mind and soul let us convey, The price that was so steep to pay, For Juneteenth's sun to light our way.

Dr. M.L.K

In the heart of Atlanta, a dream was conceived, A man, Martin Luther King, deeply believed.With faith as his armor, and love as his guide, He walked through the shadows, with no place to hide.

His voice, a powerful, mellifluous thrum,

A preacher, a prophet, from oppression he'd come.

"I Have a Dream," his echoing call, For justice, for freedom, for peace to enthrall.

He marched on 'gainst hate, on the streets paved with fears, With the weight of his people, and the strength of their tears.

A Nobel Peace Prize, the world came to see, A symbol of hope, for you and for me.

From Montgomery's bus to Birmingham's jail, His words would resound, as strong as the gale.

With nonviolent marches, he led the crusade, Against segregation, a foundation was laid.

The "Letter from Birmingham," his passionate cry, Injustice anywhere, a threat to all, nigh.

He rallied the masses, from near and from far, With dignity, grace, this bright shining star.

His life was a candle, burning so bright,

Snuffed out by darkness, in the cold April night.

But the dream of Dr. King, forever will stand,

As long as there's courage, and a reaching out hand.

For the mountaintop vision, he once had foreseen, Is a beacon for all, no matter the scene.Dr.. Martin Luther King, a name to revere, His legacy eternal, year after year.

So let this be the testament, to his sacred fight, That love conquers all, in its unstoppable might.

A preacher of peace, equality's king,

Thank you, Dr. Martin Luther King.

When the locks loosen

In concrete halls of silence deep,

Where shadows cast and sorrows weep, A soul once bound, in patience steeped,Envisions now the light of keep.

Chains of past, with time, grow weak, Walls of iron, guard no more the meek, My jail time wanes, no longer bleak, I stand before freedom's peak.

Through the bars, a glimmer breaks, A hope that stirs, as dawn awakes, Each day a step that freedom makes, To life anew, no matter what it takes.

The echo of a closing door, Resounds a promise forevermore,

That binds of old need tighten no more,As I prepare to soar.

Almost over, this sentence cast,A journey through the shadows vast, To emerge unscathed from the tempest passed, With lessons learned, held steadfast.

The light of freedom calls me near, A beacon through the last of fear, A call to step into the clear, And leave behind each fallen

Tear

.

My heart beats to a new found rhythm, Released from yesterday's darkened prism,I move ahead with optimism, To embrace life's endless spectrum.

So here I stand, at the threshold wide, With gratitude that cannot hide, For every moment, I've survived, And for the light where future abides.

Black history

In February's embrace, we pause and look back, To honor the history that textbooks might lack, A month set aside to remember and muse, Upon Black histories, triumphs, and the long-standing blues.

Black History Month, a time to reflect, On the vibrant legacies we should never neglect, From the depths of pain, through a past unjust, Rose heroes of color, in whom we trust.

They marched in stride, for rights and respect, Faced dogs and hoses, with courage unchecked,

From Rosa to Martin, they took a bold stand, And crafted a dream for a more equal land.

We echo the voices of those brilliant minds, Like Du Bois and Hughes, who brought forth new finds, In literature, science, across every field, Their quest for excellence, their right to wield.

Up, from slavery's shadow, new leaders arose, Their stories rich and deep, like a velvety rose.

Their roots run deep in the fertile soil, Their legacy lasting, despite years of toil.

Remember the soldiers, the artists, and all, Who broke through the barriers, standing so tall, Like Madame CJ Walker and Katherine Johnson's star, Who paved the way for generations afar.

A month is not enough, let's surely agree, To celebrate the depth of this history.

Yet, let this time inspire us to yearn and to learn, And to give all their stories the spotlight they earn.

For Black History is woven, a part of the quilt, Of the American saga, of blood that was spilt, Of triumph and tragedy, of poems and prose, Of the ongoing journey that onward flows.

So with every February, let's take a vow,

To remember the past, to the present, and how, Black history is made every single day, And honor its place in the American fray.

Stone walls and shattered truth

In the still of my cold, gray cell, My heart's truth, I yearn to tell, To friends and love I thought so dear, My voice, it seems, they do not hear.

With ink, my solemn words unfold,Beneath the bars where sorrows hold, I penned my need, quite clear and plain, Awaiting

warmth to ease my pain.

My so-called friend, where have you gone?

In my bleak hours, before the dawn, I asked you for a simple sum, To lighten days that have become- -

A stretch of silence, thick and grave,

No sign of the support | crave, The money for a visitor's chair, A plea for comfort in despair.

My so-called girl, our love once bright, Now shadows haunt our tender night.Each unmet call, a bitter sting, A crescendo of hope withering

.

Your silence breeds a deeper jail, Beyond the bars, my spirits fail.The echoes of my pleas return,Unanswered, as my insides churn.

Betrayal's embrace is tight and cold, Of empty promises once boldly told, Left with the ghost of your absence, A caricature of past pretense.

So here I sit in pondered thought, Lessons hard through hardship taught.The ring of truth, distinct and clear:

Support, like ghosts, just disappear.

In the company of four stark walls, The heart grows quiet, as hope befalls..For in this jail of both stone and pain, I've learned—some friendships are in vain.

Stop please don't shoot

In the heart of the night, a plea rises clear, Echoing in the alleys where the shadows peer,"Stop, please don't shoot!" a desperate cry, Begging for mercy under the gunmetal sky.

Born from fear, where innocence bleeds, A chord of humanity frantically pleads.One voice, one demand, so raw and so brash, Clamoring for life in the split second's flash.

Gun in hand, power surges in veins, A moment of choice where only fear reigns."Stop, please don't shoot!" implores the air, A future hangs trembling in the crosshairs.In a world where violence seeks to rule, Compassion's whisper is a powerful tool.

Against the noise of hatred and dispute, Resounds the charge - "Stop, please don't shoot!"Might we listen before it's too late,

To the stifled cries beneath anger's weightFor the sound of peace is a simple flute, Playing its refrain:

"Stop, please don't shoot."

Hearts pounding loudly, time slows its race, A call for reason in a darkened space.

Life's fabric so thin, easily torn and moot,

Mend it with words,

"Stop, please don't shoot."

May wisdom prevail, may we find a way, To sheath our weapons, to let love sway.

So lift up your voices, don't let them be mute, Echo together,

"Stop, please don't shoot."

For in the anthem of the living, were all a note, In the symphony of survival, we all vote.

In harmonious chorus, our fears refute,

Arms laying down to the plea,

"Stop, please don't shoot!"

Thru the veins of grief

Beneath the skies of soft twilight dew, My heart still speaks, it calls for you, A bond unbroken by earth's farewell, In whispered winds, your stories dwell.

You clothed me in love's tender thread, Wove dreams into my days, it spread Through every memory, laugh, and tear, Your voice, a lullaby, I long to hear.

Oh, Mother mine, your fight was brave, Through pain and trials, you rode each wave.

You were the warrior, fierce yet kind, A light unyielding, in darkness shined

Your name upon my trembling lips,

Each sentence paused by sorrow's grips, I need to tell you all about The days you've missed since you stepped out.

The baby boy you left behind,

Now walks the path you've surely signed, Incomplete, a jigsaw piece astray, For part of me, with you, did lay.

In moments when the silence grows, That's when my yearning for you shows.I need to feel your presence near, To guide me through each passing year.

Though cancer took you from my side, It cannot steal the love inside, A river flowing without end,A broken heart, time cannot mend.

I speak to stars, they flicker bright,"Heaven stole my guiding light,"And yet I trust, beyond blue skies, Our souls converse, in love's reprise.

I seek you in the morning's hue, In every sunset kissed with dew, A part of you, in all I see, Baby girl, you're here with me.

So rest, my angel, free from pain,

Until the day we meet again, Within my heart, your laughter stays, I am yours, in countless ways.

Two Loves, One Lesson"

He was a man split in two,
Heart tied to love he barely knew,
Two women pulling at his soul,
Each one a piece that made him whole.
Life spun fast like a wheel off track,
One wrong turn and he couldn't come back,
Cold steel bars, a slammed-shut door,
Jail made him see what he ignored before.
Inside that cell, the world kept turning,
Letters stopped, but the heart kept burning,
He heard she left, found another man—
A King in the Latin streets, part of a clan.
Word was he had problems of his own,
A shaky hand, a wounded throne,
But still, he stood where he once stood,
Taking the place he thought he never would.
And the other woman? She drifted away,
Sweet on the surface, but lies in the clay,
He learned too late what time reveals—
Some hearts are traps disguised as appeals.
Now he stands with the truth in his chest,
Knowing maybe losing them was best.
Still, it hurts—love don't fade clean,
It stains the soul like a permanent ink.
He thought maybe he'd get her back someday,
Rewrite the ending in a brand-new way,
But chances fade like smoke in the air—
Some stories end before you get there.
So he walks forward with a wiser stride,
No more shadows he tries to hide,
For the man he was died behind that wall,
And the man he is now? He won't let love fall.
Because sometimes losing what breaks you apart

Is the only way to rebuild a heart.

When Love Breaks in Two"

I was a man caught between two fires,
Two women, two dreams, two different desires.
Heart stretched thin like a wire about to snap,
Thinking I could hold it all—
Yeah... life don't work like that.
One mistake, blue lights flash,
Sirens sing, freedom crash,
Jail cell shut like the ending of a song,
And that's where I learned
Who was real...
and who been playin' me all along.
I heard she left—
Ran to another man's side,
A Latin King with a shaky hand,
Problems he could never hide.
Word on the tier was she thought he was better—
But better don't mean solid,
And solid don't mean forever.
Funny thing?
The other woman wasn't worth the chase,
Pretty smile, pretty lies,
But nothing honest in her face.
Two loves I thought I needed,
But both were just storms in disguise,
Teaching me the difference
Between real hearts... and real lies.
And me?
I sat there replaying the past,
Thinking maybe when I get out,
Maybe I still had a chance.
But dreams don't wait,
And she moved on fast—
My hope faded slow,

But my chances?
Gone just like that.
Yeah, it hurts—
Losing love, losing time, losing peace,
But sometimes God breaks you down
Just to set your spirit free.
So now I'm walking with a different kind of pride,
No more begging love to stay,
No more bleeding on the inside.
If they were meant for me,
They would've never walked away...
And if I lost 'em,
Maybe that's the blessing—
'Cause some people ain't good for your heart,
Even if you prayed they would stay.
Now I'm rebuilding from the ashes,
Stronger than I ever knew,
A man reborn from the pain—
No longer broken in two.

Sonny the Landlord"

In a small cold town where the streetlights hum,
Where December winds through the alleys drum,
Lived a landlord named Sonny with ice in his chest—
A man folk whispered never cared for the stressed.
A family lived quiet in the place they called home,
Working long hours, barely time to roam.
They fell a bit behind—just a week, maybe two—
But they scraped every dollar, did all they could do.
They reached out to Sonny with hope in their voice,
Explaining their struggle, not by greed or by choice.
But Sonny looked down with a cold, empty stare—
As if mercy was something he didn't know how to bear.
He didn't offer patience, didn't try to understand,
Didn't reach out a finger, let alone a hand.
Instead, he filed papers like tossing coal in a fire,
Fueled by ego, not need, and a heart full of ire.
The court papers came with a thud on the floor,
Stamped and official—ten days, maybe more?
No—ten days exactly to pack up their life,
A mother, kids, father—facing hardship and strife.
While Christmas lights flickered on houses nearby,
Their home became shadows, a reason to cry.
No stockings to hang, no tree glowing bright,
Just boxes and fear in the cold winter night.
Their backs to the wall, nowhere left to go,
No comfort in sight as the frost kissed the snow.
Sonny went on like he'd done something grand—
But no decent heart could ever understand.
For a man who sees dollars where compassion should be,
Is blind to the truth most good people see:
That life hits us all, and kindness is free—
A gift far more precious than rent's urgency.
And though they were pushed out into winter's embrace,

That family held tight—love their only safe place.
For a heart made of steel might win in the cold,
But a heart full of love?
That's worth more than gold.

Sonny of Pottstown"

In the town of Pottstown where the Schuylkill winds slow,
Where December paints rooftops with glimmers of snow,
Lived a landlord named Sonny, known far and around—
For owning many homes, but no heart to be found.
A family lived quiet in one of his places,
Worn-down porches, hope lit in young faces.
They paid when they could, they worked long and late,
But life hit them hard—just a little past date.
They came to him honest, voice trembling with fear,
Explaining their struggle as Christmas drew near.
But Sonny just scoffed, no compassion, no grace,
No hint of humanity shown on his face.
Instead of a chance or a little more time,
He rushed to the courthouse—cold-hearted, unkind.
Paperwork filed like it meant nothing at all,
Just numbers and names pinned up on a wall.
Then came the knock—heavy, sharp, and severe,
A notice that froze every heartbeat with fear.
Ten days to vacate. Ten days to leave.
A family in shock with no time to grieve.
No help, no guidance, no mercy in sight,
Just boxes piling up in the cold winter night.
Kids asking questions no parent could bear,
As twinkling lights mocked them everywhere.
Pottstown kept glowing with wreaths on each door,
While they packed their memories up off the floor.
Backs to the wall, no shoulder, no friend,
Just a deadline approaching the bitter year's end.
Sonny walked on like it made him a king,
Blind to the suffering his choices would bring.
For a man with no heart sees compassion as weak—
But the strongest are gentle, the brave help the meek.
And though he tossed them out in the harsh winter air,

The family held tight—love still living there.
And in that cold season, one truth stood tall:
A home built on kindness
outlasts any landlord's wall.

❄ Snow on the Windowpane ❄

A man sat quiet in the hush of night,
His chest weighed down by the world's hard bite.
Eviction papers on the table lay,
Cold as December, sharp as the day.
He tried to drown the storm within,
A cup, a swallow, the burning spin—
Hoping sleep would soften the ache,
Hoping morning might let his heart un-break.
And for a moment, drifting deep,
He let the liquor rock him to sleep.
Just a man praying for a little peace,
A little break, a small release.
But dawn arrived without permission,
Light cutting through his cloudy vision.
He rose, walked slowly to the window frame—
And the world outside was not the same.
Snow was falling, pure and white,
Dancing gentle in the new day's light.
Beautiful... yet cruel in its way,
A reminder of what could come today.
For as he watched those flakes descend,
All he saw was the fear he failed to end—
His family, cold out in that freeze,
No roof, no warmth, just winter's breeze.
And something sparked within his chest,
A stubborn fire refusing rest.
He wiped his eyes, he clenched his hands—

Because a man must rise, must stand.
"No," he whispered, fierce and low,
"My family will not walk that snow."
And though the world felt heavy still,
He found within a stronger will.
For love can lift what drink cannot,
And courage wakes when hope seems lost.
So he put the bottle down that day—
And chose instead a different way.
Out in the cold the snowfall stayed,
But inside, a vow was finally made:
He'd fight, push back, do all he could—
Because a man must shield his own from the cold,
And a father will—
When no one else would.

❄ Before the Snow Takes Us ❄

A man sat quiet in the hush of night,
His chest weighed down by the world's hard bite.
Eviction papers on the table lay,
Cold as December, sharp as the day.
He tried to drown the storm within,
A cup, a swallow, the burning spin—
Hoping sleep would soften the ache,
Hoping morning might let his heart un-break.
And for a moment, drifting deep,
He let the liquor rock him to sleep.
Just a man praying for a little peace,
A little break, a small release.
But dawn arrived without permission,
Light cutting through his cloudy vision.
He rose, walked slowly to the window frame—
And the world outside was not the same.

Snow was falling, pure and white,
Dancing gentle in the new day's light.
Beautiful... yet cruel in its way,
A reminder of what could come today.
For as he watched those flakes descend,
All he saw was the fear he failed to end—
His family, cold out in that freeze,
No roof, no warmth, just winter's breeze.
And something sparked within his chest,
A stubborn fire refusing rest.
He wiped his eyes, he clenched his hands—
Because a man must rise, must stand.
"No," he whispered, fierce and low,
"My family will not walk that snow."
And though the world felt heavy still,
He found within a stronger will.
For love can lift what drink cannot,
And courage wakes when hope seems lost.
So he put the bottle down that day—
And chose instead a different way.
Out in the cold the snowfall stayed,
But inside, a vow was finally made:
He'd fight, push back, do all he could—
Because a man must shield his own from the cold,
And a father will—
When no one else would.

I'm So Harlem

I'm so Harlem—
Raised by cracked sidewalks and loud laughs,
Where the stoops tell stories
And the streets remember names.
I'm so Harlem—

Church hats on Sunday,
Hustle Monday through Friday,
Dreams tucked in coat pockets
Against the cold.
I'm so Harlem—
Jazz in my heartbeat,
Hip-hop in my walk,
Soul food wisdom
Passed down without recipes.
I learned strength from grandmothers
With tired hands and unbreakable backs,
From men who spoke little
But stood tall through storms.
I'm so Harlem—
Where pain made poets,
And struggle taught style,
Where we turn scars into art
And survival into swagger.
I'm the echo of Apollo lights,
The rhythm of late-night trains,
The hope that never packed up
Even when the rent came due.
I'm so Harlem—
Still proud, still rising,
Still gold under pressure.
No matter where I stand in this world,
Harlem stands in me.

New Year, No More Bullshit

New year—
out with the phoniness,
out with the fuckery,
out with fake smiles and borrowed stories.
I'm done watching silver-spoon babies
play gangster for applause,
wearing pain like a costume
they can take off at night.
You never missed a meal
but talk like hunger raised you.
Never ducked a bill
but swear the streets made you.
That ain't struggle—
that's theater.
This year, we telling the truth loud.
Respect earned, not rented.
Scars real, not captioned.
If you ain't bled for it,
don't preach it.
I salute the ones who came up cold,
who learned survival before success,
who know silence sometimes screams louder
than any flex online.
New year—
I'm trimming the circle,
cutting off the noise,
choosing substance over shine.
No more cosplaying pain.
No more fake kings.
If you ain't built from the mud,
don't track dirt in my house.
This year is for growth,
for real ones only,
for moving forward

without carrying other people's lies.
New year.
New energy.
Same truth.

Don't miss out!

Visit the website below and you can sign up to receive emails whenever DARRYL"BOTTEGA BOY DEE"JONES publishes a new book. There's no charge and no obligation.

https://books2read.com/r/B-A-NDEKE-RPYTG

BOOKS 2 READ

Connecting independent readers to independent writers.

www.ingramcontent.com/pod-product-compliance
Lightning Source LLC
LaVergne TN
LVHW052320200926
848481LV00002B/620